CUSTOMERS FOR LIFE

Tips, Techniques and Strategies for Growing ANY Business Even In the Toughest Economy

Brian Carson

ISBN: 0615833136
ISBN-13: 978-0615833132

Dedicated to:
Rex, Missy, Becca and Matt. My Naylor & Associates comrades who actually put up with my dark sense of humor. To my brother Dave who has been a huge influence on me.

And to my wife, Maria. She is my best friend, my soul mate and my better half.

Contents

Introduction

If someone could wave a magic wand and suddenly change something about your chosen profession or business, what one thing would you have them change?

Would you have them provide you with an easier way to contact better qualified prospects? Would you want those prospects and your current customers to view you as a true professional, or maybe even an "expert" in your field?

You may be good now, but how would you like to be even better at making more effective, more persuasive presentations? Perhaps you would like to be better at closing sales or handling objections. Or, is repeat business more important to you?

What if your current customers felt you were the only person or the only business that understood and could serve their specialized, unique and individual needs?

How about referrals? Take the best customer you have right now. How would you like more contacts just like them than you could handle? What one thing would you change to make you a better, happier, and more productive businessperson?

In the chapters to follow, we'll be discussing not only these areas, but other factors critical for you to realize real business success. Throughout the pages of this book, we'll explore some of the most effective ideas, field proven methods and techniques you can use immediately to help you increase your sales, improve your business, overcome your most difficult problems and challenges, gain extra income, have more free time, and find a renewed enjoyment from your chosen business.

Increasing Your Effectiveness

It's no secret that things are changing today, faster than ever before. Technology has become more sophisticated, competition more keen, and consumers – the people who buy your products and services – are more educated and aware.

And with the wide variety of choices your customers or clients have, not only in similar products and services from different companies, but also in the individual people they deal with, the more skillful and professional you are at meeting your customer's needs, the bigger advantage you can command, and the more effective and successful you can become.

If you want to be effective and successful in the marketplace today, it is necessary, even vital, that you continually change, improve, adjust and update your selling, service, and problem-solving skills, and your methods of marketing and general business operation. It has been said, (and you've no doubt heard) that:

**"People don't care how much you know,
until they know how much you care."**

One of the best and most effective ways you can show your prospects and customers you care, is by helping them solve their problems in a satisfactory, cost-effective, and professional manner.

Exposure to New Ideas

And that's what this book is all about. It's written with the goal of helping you become the best you can be at what you do professionally.

Naturally, this program doesn't claim, nor does it pretend to have all the answers to all your business problems. No book, course or seminar could do that.

Rather, the objective of the book is to expose you to some tried, tested, and field proven ideas, concepts, and techniques that work for other business people much like you.

Once acquainted with new information and ideas, it will be up to you to decide which ideas can best be tailored to your own individual business situation, and how you will use them to serve your customers and prospects better.

The goal of this book is not to make you a marketing expert, but to provide you with some tools the experts and those who succeed in business are using.

Together, we'll explore specific marketing, sales, customer service, and business building techniques others used to significantly increase their businesses and incomes with little extra effort.

You'll most likely find that many of these ideas will be easy to implement, and you'll be able to use them right away. Others may take a little longer to gear up for. Still others may not be right for you or your operation. That's okay. It's not possible to provide 100% usable ideas for every person in every situation.

However, if you get just one or two good, usable ideas you can put into your business operation that makes a difference, then your time, effort and money will be well invested.

How We Retain Information

Getting a new idea is one thing, but what you do with it once you have it is just as important as getting it. Studies on retention show you remember:

- 10% of what you read,

- 22% of what you hear,

- 37% of what you see,

- 56% of what you see and hear, and up to

- 86% of what you see, hear and do.

So an idea heard but not acted on is only half as likely retained as an idea put into practice. With that concept in mind, if the information in this book is to be of any real value to you, it must not only be read, it must be applied. It must be experienced, or acted on. And that means it will take effort on your part.

In their book, **The Knowing-Doing Gap,** authors, Jeffrey Pheffer and Robert L. Sutton mention that every year there are 1,700 new business books published, $60 billion spent on training, $43 billion spent on consultants and our universities turn out 80,000 graduates with MBA's. Yet, most businesses continue to operate day in and day out in much the same way they've always done.

Knowledge without action is no better than no knowledge at all. Just knowing isn't enough. You've got to do something with what you know.

The ideas in this book work. They're not theory. They're not speculation on what "should" work. And they're not philosophical musings. These ideas, concepts and techniques are in use by business owners across the country in one form or another. They're being proven in actual field use day in and day out.

They work for others, and they can work for you. But, take the time to study them, understand them and make the modifications to tailor them to your own personal and business style and operation. And then finally, apply them in your business.

Five Steps of Learning and Retention

Learning – the acquisition of new information or knowledge, and Retention – the ability to capture that information and recall it when wanted or needed, is actually a process that involves five steps:

First, is **Impact?** Receiving the idea in your mind. Impact can be in a word, a visual observation or a concept. It makes no difference. Your mind isn't capable of distinguishing between a visual and an actual experience. Nor is it capable of determining the difference between a conscious and an unconscious impact an idea may have on you. As far as your mind is concerned, those experiences are all the same and your mind will accept them, regardless.

If information or an experience appears real to your mind your emotions and nervous system will react as though it were real.

To illustrate this point, try this simple experiment:

Seat yourself in a comfortable chair, feet flat on the floor and your hands resting comfortably in your lap.

Close your eyes, take a deep breath, let it out slowly and relax. Take another one. Let it out slowly. Relax even more.

Picture a lemon resting on a table in front of you. Visualize it. See it clearly. Look at its shape – its color – its texture.

Now, mentally reach out with your hand and pick up the lemon. Bring it up to your face. Look at it closely. Squeeze it. Do you notice how firm it feels? Feel the texture of the lemon's dimply and waxy skin. Notice the lemon's yellow color and round shape, with its pointy ends.

Now, hold it up to your nose. Smell it. Do you notice the lemon's citrusy smell?

Place the lemon on the table and mentally pick up a knife that's lying nearby. Cut the lemon in two.

Pick up one half of the lemon and see the juice dripping from it. Bring the lemon up to your nose. Smell it again. Now bite into the lemon.

What's happening to you right now? Is saliva flooding your mouth, both in your mind, and physically?

Now consider what just happened. In actuality, there was no lemon. You just pictured one in your mind. While this was just a mental exercise, and the lemon was just imagined, chances are, if you are like most people, the mental image you were playing on the screen of your mind triggered certain responses, which manifested themselves physically. So, you can see by this demonstration, that *Impact*, is a critical step involved in learning and retention.

The second step is **Repetition.** One university study revealed an idea read or heard only one time was 66% forgotten within 24 hours. But if that same idea was read or heard repeatedly for eight days, up to 90% of it could be retained at the end of the eight days.

So once you've read this book all the way through, go back and read it again. But this time read with a highlighter, a pencil and notepad handy. Mark up the book. Write down the ideas you feel fit your personal business situation. This repetition will help you retain more of the information than if you had read it only once.

The third step in the learning and retention process is **Utilization.** This is the "doing" step. Here neuromuscular pathways are developed, creating a "mind-muscle memory." And according to the study quoted earlier, once you physically experience an action, it becomes twice as easy to recall as if you had heard it only.

Fourth, is **Internalization.** Making the idea a part of you. That may involve some customizing or tailoring of the idea to fit your situation or style, but it is vitally important for you to personalize the idea and make it "yours."

The fifth step is **Reinforcement.** To maximize the effectiveness of an idea, continually be looking for ways to support and strengthen it. The more you can support the idea, the more you will believe it, the longer you will retain it, and the more effective it will become in helping you serve your customers' needs.

Now, what does all this have to do with your business? Simply this. In your daily business and personal activities, and throughout your experience with the information in this book, you will be exposed to many ideas.

Some will be brand new; you've never heard them before. Some will be ideas you have heard in the past, but have forgotten. And others will be ideas you come up with on your own because of something that was triggered in your mind as you read. Understanding and applying these five steps in the learning and retention process can help you retain more of what you read and experience.

Action Makes the Difference

It's important to keep an open mind as you read, hear, or otherwise experience ideas that can help you. Try not to judge them or cast them aside too quickly because they don't sound good, they're not part of your personality or make-up, or you may have heard them before.

Instead, consider this course of action:

If you've heard an idea before, say to yourself, "Yes, I've heard that before, but am I using it?" If not, "Why not?"

If you are using the idea, ask yourself, "How effective am I at using it? How can I 'plus', or improve on it to make it even more effective for me and my business?"

Next, ask yourself this question: "What will I do as a result of what I've learned?"

Remember, it's not *what* you know – it's what you *do* that counts. Ideas are powerful. And good ideas are important for any business. They're what keep your interest up and your business fresh, alive, and growing. And put into action, good ideas can make a huge difference in the way you do business, the results you realize, the fun you have, and the profits you make.

This book is full of good, practical, and usable ideas that can help make that big difference for you. But it's up to you to tailor them to your own unique situation, and to put them into action.

The Business You're In

If you don't learn another thing from our time together, remember this…

**You're NOT in the (Whatever business you're in) business…
You're in the _MARKETING_ business.**

Read that sentence again… and again… and again. Digest it. Understand it. Internalize it. Make it an integral part of your business philosophy. Because unless you do, your business will be no better and no different from any of the other choices your prospects and customers can select to do business with.

Let me explain by using the insurance profession as an example, and as I do, think about how these principles might apply to your business.

It's a well-known fact that very few people (if any at all), want to buy an insurance policy. It's true, they may want the benefits, security and peace of mind that the insurance provides them and their families or their business, but they don't want to spend their money on an insurance policy. But, what do most insurance people sell?

They sell insurance!

No wonder the business is so difficult. It takes no Harvard degree to figure it out. If you sell insurance… and know that people don't want to buy insurance… why would you continue to beat your head against the wall trying to sell it?

Consider the way most people shop for auto insurance. They call up several insurance companies and ask for a quote. The agent asks what coverage the caller is carrying, and gives a quote based on those figures.

The caller then thanks the agent, and goes to the next number on their list. They keep repeating the scenario until they're convinced they've found the lowest price… and whichever company comes in lowest gets the business.

But, wait a minute. Isn't there more to buying insurance than just "low price?" Well, sure there is. And you and I both know it. And so do most insurance agents.

Why is it nearly every agent from nearly every insurance company you call tries to sell on price… knowing that there's probably someone out there with a price lower than they can quote?

Why is it so few agents try to differentiate themselves from their competition, and change the prospect's base of thinking away from price, and on to other, more important things?

Price is important, very important. And it carries a lot of weight in a prospect's buying decision.

But it's only one of many factors a person must consider when making their buying decision.

In actuality, there's little difference in insurance policies issued by many insurance companies in the same geographical area.

Likewise, there's usually little difference in the products or services you sell versus those same types of products or services sold by your competitors.

General overhead costs, utilities, phones, supplies, wages, and product costs are also similar for most companies that sell like products and services.

So, if all those factors… similarity of products and services, overhead costs and product costs… are the same, the prices charged by each individual business must, out of necessity, be close.

It's true that one company may obtain a lower purchase price on their products and be able to offer a more attractive sales price for a certain period, but eventually, things change and the playing field becomes level once again.

There are other factors not to be overlooked such as investment income and tax write-offs or advantages that can play a role in the prices businesses charge for the things they sell.

Overall, all things considered, the prices charged for the goods and services from one company to another similar company will be fairly close over the long haul.

The point is,… no matter what business you're in…

**You will never maintain, long-term…
a competitive advantage because
of the products you offer, or
the prices you charge.**

As soon as you develop a new product, or offer a new service, it's just a matter of time before your competition latches on to it and offers the exact same thing, or maybe enhances it and offers it for a lower price. And as soon as you lower your prices, your competition can do the same thing.

The marketplace you operate in is so fiercely competitive… so cutthroat… so unforgiving… that you absolutely *must* differentiate yourself from your competition.

If you don't, you'll be relegated to just another "me-too" business, just like all your competitors.

Now… want to know the good news?

That's how your competitors operate… in a "ME-TOO!" mode.

Just look around. They're all the same. Their businesses all look the same. Their products are all the same. They walk and talk the same. And their advertising all looks like and says the same thing as the next guy. Because they all operate that way and don't know how to change… it gives you a tremendous opportunity!

If they keep on doing what they've always done… they'll keep on getting what they've always got.

But you… if you want to get something different… you've got to be willing to make changes. And that's what this program is all about. Making changes… changes that will produce real and measurable results in your business.

But, what you'll learn here isn't enough. These ideas and strategies alone, won't work. You've got to take action on them, if you expect anything different from what you're getting.

So, make the action commitment now… and let's get started!

1

Achieving Outstanding Business Success

Personal Traits of Exceptional Performers

Some time back a young entrepreneur had the pleasant opportunity of having dinner with Earl Nightingale, the famous radio personality and producer of self improvement programs.

Earl made his life's work studying successful people and how they achieved their successes.

The young entrepreneur had long admired Earl for his ideas and philosophy.

And on that occasion, he asked him what advice Earl would give his young son if he had one. What, based on his vast experience and knowledge, would be the one thing that would help his son ensure success both in business and in his personal life?

Earl told the young businessman, "You know, I have often thought about that very question. And after all the years and all the study, I've come to the conclusion that your success in life, or in business for that matter, can be boiled down to one thing. Your rewards will always be in direct proportion to the service you render and the value you create for others.

"You only have to look around," he said. "The people who serve others prosper. The people who don't serve others will not prosper. And you can tell just how successful a person is, by the service they render to others.

"The problem," he continued, "is that unsuccessful people either haven't learned that great secret, or they don't apply it.

"The successful people are the ones who develop the habits of doing the things that unsuccessful people don't do for one reason or another."

What Failures Don't Like to Do

Earl's comments hit the young entrepreneur like a big hammer that night, as he realized how true they were. The more you serve your customers, and help them satisfy their needs, the more you will prosper.

And as a business owner, business manager, professional person or entrepreneur, serving your customer's needs means you must do the things unsuccessful business owners, managers, professionals, and entrepreneurs don't do.

There is no doubt it is difficult to work long hours or on

weekends when your family is waiting for you at home, and be stood up for an appointment someone made with you.

It's tough to make telephone calls, only to be met with hostile and rude people on the other end who curse at you or slam the phone down.

It's discouraging to set goals, schedule interviews, explain the technical aspects and benefits of the products and services you provide, overcome customer's objections and misconceptions, and give exceptional service, only to have your customer go elsewhere because they found the same product or service for a few dollars less.

Enough of these experiences can discourage anyone. And after a while, some people just quit trying. They find it easier to adjust their standard of living downward to match their income than to adjust their income upward to create their desired standard of living.

They are no longer in control. Inflation dictates the price of things they buy, and competition and luck determine how much they have to spend. Fortunately, for them, many of their competitors are in the same situation.

Outstanding success is unusual, and depends on many factors. For some people, it just happens. They're in the right place at the right time, they do nothing special, and everything just falls into place for them. Others put in long hours and much work, only to find average success.

But a clear understanding of success principles, a well-developed and executed plan, and certain personal traits and characteristics can help move you towards your goals more quickly.

Here are some personal qualities to consider:

Eight Personal Qualities for Success

1. Know What You Want

Know yourself and exactly what you want and expect out of your business. So many people enter business and spend years in that environment having no idea of what they want, or what is possible to get out of their business. And it's no different in any profession.

Most business owners are working so hard *in* their businesses they don't have time to work *on* it. They've become slaves to their business. They've got things backwards. They're working for their business rather than their business working for them.

Take the time to carefully analyze where you've come from, where you are now, and what you want to accomplish in your business, your job or your career. Then set some meaningful goals to help you accomplish your objectives. If you don't know where you want to go, you'll not understand what to do to get there.

Meaningful goals are an essential requirement for success in business. With goals, you have a target to aim for, a purpose for being, and a direction to travel. Without goals, it's easy to wander aimlessly, getting sidetracked with any little thing that comes along.

When you set your goals, think of the word, "SMART." Have SMART goals. Your goals should be:

- Specific,
- Measurable,
- Attainable,
- Realistic, and

- Time-bound

It is important for your goals to be *Specific,* so you will know exactly what you're shooting for. Your goal should be clearly defined and identified so you not only know what you are trying to accomplish, but when you've achieved it.

If you say, "I want to sell more products, merchandise or services or reduce the number of contacts to close a sale." That isn't enough. You need to clearly specify your goal. Is it 12 more sales per month? An extra $100,000 in monthly sales? How about a certain amount of products or services? How much – specifically?

Whatever your goal, there should be no doubt about what you wish to accomplish.

Your goals should be *Measurable.* There should be a system, or method of determining how you are progressing in your efforts for attainment. By clearly defining your goals as discussed in the previous step, you will be more able to measure them. It's important for you to see your current status, and progression towards your goals.

Next, your goals should be *Attainable.* If your goal is too high… if there's no hope for you to reach it, it won't take long for you to become discouraged, and you will either lose concentration and the drive to pursue your goal, or you will abandon it altogether.

Your goal should be something you can reach with just a little extra effort. After you gain confidence, then go after the big hairy audacious goals.

An insurance agency owner I'm acquainted with had a large fire and casualty agency. To promote the sale of life insurance to his on-board customers, the agency owner introduced a contest for his agents. The agent who sold the most life insurance would win a trip to Hawaii.

One of the agents who worked for the agency but who had never sold much life insurance, decided he wanted to win the trip. The qualifications to earn the trip were tough, and based entirely on the sale of life insurance.

Very few agents in this agency ever earned these types of trips by working the entire year for them, but this agent put his mind to it and qualified in only four months.

Considering the agent's past performance regarding life insurance production, it's questionable whether the goal should have been attainable for him. However, the agent found a motivation within that changed the odds to his favor, and he could accomplish in a four-month period what most agents weren't able to do in an entire year.

In your business operation you need to make sure your goals are not only attainable, but are also…

Realistic. If your goal isn't realistic, if it's not something within your realm of achievement, it's just a matter of time before you'll become frustrated and give up. And that can have a negative effect on you as you think of yourself as a failure, or not being good at setting goals.

Then, because of your negative image of yourself relative to setting goals, you will likely give up setting goals. It's a self-feeding mechanism.

The key to being good at setting and achieving goals is to be realistic in your expectations. Set attainable and realistic goals that can be reached with a little effort.

That builds a success image, and enhances your self-confidence in a positive way. Then, the next time, set a little higher goal. Again, one you know you can achieve. And that adds on to, and builds your confidence that much more.

The next step is to make your goals, *Time-bound.* Set a time limit for their attainment.

This helps you keep on target, not be distracted, and encourages you to complete something you've started. Not only will this help you to realize success at a pre-designated time, but you will enhance your self-image by accomplishing your goal.

If, for instance, your goal is to sell some a certain product or service, or a pre-determined dollar amount of sales this year, break that number down into months, weeks, and even days, if necessary.

A large goal becomes much more manageable in small pieces. The key is to break your goals into bite-size pieces, and place a time deadline on them for their accomplishment.

2. The Ability to Focus

The second quality is the ability to focus. Many people hesitate to go into business because they think they lack the talents and abilities to succeed. They look at others who succeed and think they must have unique talents or capabilities. But after getting to know that person they find them to be average.

The main difference is the successful person has developed the ability to focus. A person of average intelligence, who is focused on a specific goal, will consistently outperform the brightest people not focused on anything specific.

3. Determine the Price You'll Pay

You must determine the price you must pay to succeed. For everything in life, there is a price. And it must be paid before you can realize the rewards. Often it takes sacrifice.

A few years ago, to get a little exercise and help relieve stress, one of my friends bought matching bicycles for him and his wife. They had fun for a while, but then a group of experienced riders flew by him one day on their fast, shiny high-priced racing bikes.

Always a competitive person, my friend decided he would try to catch them and ride with them. But, try as he might, it was to no avail. Nothing he did would allow him to catch up to them. That ate on my friend for about a week, and it wasn't long before he found himself back in the bike shop getting the specifications and prices of one of those "fast, shiny, obviously high-priced" bikes.

And so $2,500 later, he was back on the road just waiting for those riders to catch him so he could ride with them. My friend was decked out in cycling shorts and jersey, special shoes, helmet and his new 16-speed racer.

Then one day it happened. The group of riders came up on my friend from behind, and he was determined to keep up with them. But a quarter of a mile later, try as he might, he was "off the back." The riders were gone, never to be seen again. That irritated my friend.

So he bought several books, obtained video tapes, and sought the help of a neighbor who was a good rider. He worked hard trying to develop his cycling abilities. He rode every morning from 4:30 to 7:30, while his family was still asleep.

My friend encountered motorists who didn't like cyclists. Some even ran him off the road and throw bottles at him.

He's ridden in the rain and cold weather, and in the 120-degree heat. My friend worked hard and eventually hired a cycling coach to help him develop his skills.

Then he entered a local race, and to his surprise, he won! This encouraged him so he entered another race. Then another, and another, and he just kept winning.

With the new skills and confidence he was developing, he entered the state and national championships, placing high in both. The riders who used to pass him were now coming to him for help and advice. They wondered how he could consistently beat them when he hadn't been riding for nearly as long as they had.

They didn't understand it wasn't how long my friend had been training, as much as what he had put into his training.

It wasn't what he did during the race that counted as much as it was what he did during the long, lonely, solitary hours of training.

It was the sacrifices he made that made the difference between being a social rider, or the national champion he'll eventually become.

The same concept of sacrifice applies to operating a successful business.

If you want to reap the great and abundant rewards your business can provide you, you will have to do not-so-glamorous things at some not-so-convenient times.

You're going to do what Earl Nightingale said... you must do "...the things that unsuccessful business owners don't want to do."

That may mean, depending on the business you have or operate, you must leave the comfort of your store or office to visit with people about their needs in their homes or businesses at inconvenient times.

If you have a family, this may prove to be a hardship on you, but if you are just starting out in business, or want to increase your existing business or achieve some new goals, you may have to make that sacrifice.

If you are not willing to make the sacrifices, then you can't expect to be as successful in business as someone who will make those sacrifices.

4. Self Responsibility

You are responsible for the success of your business and

your life. There are no excuses. There may be setbacks or economic downturns, or problems that affect your business.

Your suppliers or vendors may discontinue making or providing your favorite products or services, change the way they do business with you or even merge with another company.

Economies change, corporate policies change, and prospects don't buy from you, and the weather is too hot or too cold.

While those things definitely affect you, the way you do business and the sales you make, those things are beyond your control, and it's up to you, and you alone, to accept responsibility for the success of your business.

No matter how bad you might have it, no matter what difficulties or challenges you might encounter, let me assure you there are many people who have had difficulties and challenges far greater than any you are ever likely to encounter, and somehow, they pull through. And you can do the same.

Here's a little credo that can help you. It contains just ten, two-letter words:

"If it is to be, it is up to me."

That simple one line sentence says it all. It places the responsibility exactly where it should be... *directly on your shoulders.*

5. Be Committed

Make a total commitment to your success. Once you have decided to be in business, be in that business.

Get into it with both feet. Don't let anything hold you back.

Even more than getting in the business, see that the business gets in you.

Make a commitment you will succeed, no matter what.

Don't try to work two jobs or projects at one time. You can't do either of them justice, and you'll likely end up frustrated and broke, and never know whether you could have succeeded.

6. The Extra Mile

The sixth personal quality to achieve outstanding success in business is that you must go the extra mile.

It's the "Under promise, over deliver" concept, and can be summed up in the following statement:

"If you are always willing to do more than what you get paid for, the day will come when you will be paid for more than what you actually do."

Robert Cialdini, in his book, *Influence: The Psychology of Persuasion*, discusses what he calls the Law of Reciprocity. Basically, it says that when you do something for someone else there's an unstated obligation for them to want to do something for you in return.

So, when you go the extra mile for your customers or clients, you've just set the stage for that law to take effect. But it's only on that "extra mile" this works. When you give what might be considered "normal" service, or "adequate" service or – even "good" service, you haven't earned the right to expect that law to work for you.

Even performing "knock-out" service often isn't enough to gain you an advantage. We've all come to expect that from all businesses.

You really have to do something special to gain an advantage in today's highly competitive marketplace. Then, and only then, can you expect to create that nearly compelling desire in your customer to want to reciprocate. This simple truth says it all:

"There's no traffic jam along the extra mile."

7. Control Your Time

The seventh quality is that you must master and take control of your time. Time is an expendable commodity. Each one of us has the same 24 hours in each day. When those hours are gone, they cannot be replaced. They are gone forever, never to be recaptured.

You must treat your time as precious, and guard it wisely and selfishly. Don't let anyone disrupt you or take you away from the focus on your goals.

People who don't have goals are used by people who do. If you let others draw you away from your goals, you simply say that their goals are more important than your own.

If you are serious about business success – really serious, then this is one of the most important and critical areas to defend.

8. *Persistence and Determination*

Number eight, is to develop persistence and determination. Occasionally you will encounter setbacks or reach plateaus where it seems like nothing is going right.

Your competitors lower their prices, run massive ad campaigns and unheard of promotions, and the next thing you know your customers and clients do business with them.

Business is walking out the back door faster than it's coming in the front door.

Your volume is dropping, and you become concerned.

You seem to spend more time in a defensive posture than you do in servicing your existing customers, and you're losing.

Now is not the time to give up. Now is the time to dig in and play offensively.

To be determined not to lose your good customers – the ones you worked so hard to get. Your strategy should be to keep in touch with them and continue providing exceptional service.

Nearly every business is cyclical. Eventually things will change.

While you can't be competitive on price all the time, you can be competitive on the service you give, and the empathy for your customers and their problems.

We'll talk more about how to do that in a later chapter, but for now, just resolve in advance; no matter what, you'll never give up.

Six Personal Abilities Help Guarantee Results

Besides those eight personal qualities, six additional abilities can help you achieve even greater success:

1. Effective Communication

First, is the ability to communicate effectively with others. You must be able to interact with other people on their level, so they understand you and the points you are trying to get across to them.

Remember that everyone is different. Each of us have different communication and behavior styles, and you need to be versatile enough to relate to each person according to their individual style. Be careful that you speak language they are familiar with and can relate to, and that you don't overuse "buzz words," or industry jargon.

2. Stay on Target

This is the ability for you to quickly make midstream corrections. Each one of us is human, and is subject to the frailties that accompany this mortal life. Occasionally, we all make mistakes or errors in judgment.

Making the mistake or the error is not the problem – the first time. It's when we keep making the same mistakes repeatedly, without learning from them, or that we fail to quickly recover and make the corrections to avoid total calamity, that we run into problems.

3. Develop Foresight

The ability to spot and analyze trends. To look at the past and what is happening today, and predict what might happen, can have a significant impact on your business success. Another word for this skill is "foresight."

In a recent interview, the president of a very large meat company told how just a few years ago, their largest selling items were canned hams. But today, with more women working, and less time to spend in the kitchen, they sell very few canned hams.

Today their mainstay is precooked dinners. Without foresight, or the ability to look ahead and predict with reasonable accuracy what may happen in the near future, a company could lose its competitive position and find itself in serious trouble.

As a business owner, give serious thought to keeping abreast of industry changes, new laws, tax laws, buying trends, and other factors that could affect your customers either positively or negatively. Then take whatever steps are necessary to prepare yourself to address those changes, and posture yourself in the minds of your customers as the expert they've come to know and depend on.

4. Demonstrate Leadership

The fourth ability or skill to develop for outstanding success is that of leadership. Leadership is the ability to take charge and move others to action.

When working with a prospect, client or customer, and have identified and analyzed their needs, it is up to you to prepare and recommend a good, workable plan or proposal that will help satisfy those needs; a plan that's right for their situation and that fits their budget.

It's not up to the customer to tell you what they want. You are the professional. They have come to you for help and advice. You've got a lot more experience, knowledge and understanding of your products and services and what they can do for them than they do. It is up to you to take charge and assume responsibility for the satisfaction and solving of their problems, needs and wants.

And if you approach it with the right mix of professionalism, knowledge and confidence you'll be amazed at how many people will take your advice and follow your leadership.

5. Persuasive Selling Skills

The ability to sell well. It's surprising how little most people in business know about professional selling. Selling is one of the most important skills you as a professional business person can possess.

Many of your prospects and your existing customers know just enough about what your products or services can do for them to be dangerous. They have talked to other people, read a few articles in some magazines, may even have seen a program or two on television, checked things out on the Internet, and they think they know exactly what they need. Sometimes they may be close.

But in other cases, they're far from the mark. You owe it to your customers to be as effective a salesperson as you can be. By doing that, you'll give better solutions and better value, saving them both time and money, and helping them have greater piece of mind knowing they have the products or services best for them.

They will also feel good about their choice of a place of business, knowing they have just dealt with real professionals who really care about them.

You will be a beneficiary of that effort, too. You will you feel good about yourself and the job you have just done for your customer and that will cause you to be more effective and professional in your next interview or sale. Not only that, but your customer, being satisfied with what you have done for him or her, will be more inclined to tell others of their experience.

Believe me, people respond to the personal experiences of people they respect. And they'll respond to you, because a real professional and caring person or business is hard to find these days.

6. Action

The sixth ability to develop is that of action. All the things we've discussed in this chapter will do you, nor anyone else (your customers, for instance) any good if you don't take action and do something about them.

Remember, action is the key. It's not what you know, it's not what you talk about, it's what you do. True success in business, or in life, is an ongoing process. As Joel Weldon says,

"The Road to Success is Always Under Construction."

Some people say that knowledge is power. But it isn't. Knowledge is not power unless it's applied. This chapter has supplied you with some vital knowledge to be successful in business. You now have the knowledge – now it's up to you to put that knowledge into action.

BRIAN CARSON

"Laughter is the shortest distance between two people."

Victor Borge

2

How Do Your Customers See You?

Establishing a Positive Identity in the Minds of Your Customers

Think of the word, "Professional." What image comes to your mind? Do you visualize a doctor, a dentist, a lawyer, or perhaps the president of a large corporation?

Did the image of the owner or manager of the business you operate cross your mind?

What criteria do you use to define a "professional?"

What about other people – your customers, for example?

How do you think they define a "professional?"

The services you perform for your customers daily can have a big impact on them, their family, their staff, employees or customers if they have businesses, and their financial futures.

The way you run your business and handle your customers' needs daily says a lot about you and the position you occupy in their minds.

Your occupation should be viewed as being just as "professional" as that of any other, including doctors, dentists, lawyers, or any other business head.

The critical question is, how professionally do you perform within your occupation?

While this program is not a sales training course, it's important to know that no matter what your role in business is, you're involved in sales in one form or another.

And if you have staff or employees involved in sales, it's important for you to know the following information.

Five Types of Salespeople

Just as different salespeople have their own different and unique personalities, they also have different skill levels for selling and servicing their customers.

As we discuss the various types of salespeople and classify them according to their skill level, you will no doubt recognize people you know or encountered in the past. And as we do, take an honest look at yourself, to see where you might fit.

Professional Visitor

This person has no problem making appointments. They thrive on it. They enjoy visiting and talking to people, getting to know them, and may even engage in a casual discussion of their customers' problems.

Their conversation with a customer or prospect may or may not eventually involve the subject of how their products or services can benefit the buyers, and if it does, it usually has to be instigated by the customer or prospect.

A typical sales presentation will be oral, with little (if any) use of visual materials, product brochures, or printed proposals.

Order Taker

These people don't mind talking to customers, clients or prospects, if they don't have to initiate the call. They are uncomfortable making appointments, and would rather have the customer or prospect come to them.

The telephone presents just as much a problem for these people. If the phone rings, they'll take the call and even discuss the customer's needs. But it's tough for them to pick up the receiver and dial a customer's number.

They operate best from a base of "low price," and have difficulty handling objections. They would rather wait until someone asks for something specific, then they have no trouble filling the order.

Peddler

These are "sales-oriented" people. They have good product knowledge, but severely lack in "people skills." They operate from a "hit-and-run" approach.

This person will assume a certain level of product knowledge by the customer, and establish rapport with them. These people are "product-oriented," or "price-oriented." Their entire presentation is based on product features or price, with little regard to how the product or service will benefit the customer.

The Peddler is the most prevalent salesperson you will find. Telemarketers who work the consumer market fit nicely into this category. It seems like it never fails. You may have just gotten home from a tough day at work and are relaxing with the kids, working in the yard, or perhaps even eating dinner.

Then the phone rings. It's for you. The individual on the other end dives right into their presentation with no regard for whom they're calling.

For most people, especially professional salespeople, this inconvenience and the salesperson's level of incompetence are most aggravating. In these types of calls, the salesperson shows no concern for the prospect's time, inconvenience, present level of product knowledge, or whether or not there's any level of need, want or desire to know more about what they're selling.

The assumption is made by the caller that what he or she is offering the prospect in a product, service or convenience is the same or better than what the prospect has, and all the prospect is interested in is price. This approach is an insult to the prospect or customer, and is one of the biggest mistakes a salesperson can make.

The do-not-call list has stopped a lot of this nonsense, but not as much as we originally thought.

Problem Solver

These salespeople enjoy getting in front of people, ferreting out problems, needs and wants, and discussing workable solutions. They have empathy for the customer, can see the customer's needs *from the customer's point of view,* and enjoy helping the customer solve their problems.

The problem-solving person is good at establishing rapport with the prospect or customer, identifying what their needs, wants and desires are, developing creative, needs and wants satisfying proposals, and making effective presentations.

But when it comes time to ask for the order, or close the sale, they tense up, lose their confidence, or otherwise fail to close the sale. Their customers or prospects, now having their needs identified and solutions presented, go elsewhere looking for a "better buy."

This salesperson has done all the work, and an Order Taker for another company gets the sale – and the commission. After the Peddler, this is the next most common salesperson.

Counselor

In the business world, it's not uncommon for companies and corporations to have a staff of lawyers, or "legal counsel," on retainer to give advice in matters pertaining to the law, taxes, investments, mergers, or other difficult or legal situations.

The Counselor knows that for important buying decisions, his or her customers, be they companies, corporations, or individuals, should be no different.

To them, buying any product or service is a serious matter, not to be taken lightly, and can be an important tool for solving a need, satisfying a problem or adding to their profits, convenience or lifestyle.

They know that their customers need professional and qualified representation and advice, and the Counselor will do whatever it takes to provide it for them.

Like corporate legal counsel, this salesperson postures him or herself as being "on retainer," always available to give advice on matters pertaining to the products or services they sell. They clarify it in the customer's mind there is absolutely no need for them to go anywhere else for answers to the problems their products or services can solve.

The Counselor knows how to establish rapport, build professional trust and credibility, identify their customer's current problems, develop effective proposals, offer credible and workable solutions, and make the presentation so their customers have no question in their minds they must buy the concepts they present, and hence, the product or service.

In addition, they can point out other, potential problems the customer might encounter, and help them solve those needs.

This person operates much like a professional billiards champion. Before each shot, the billiards champion will carefully analyze the layout of the balls on the table, to see where the next two or three shots can best be made.

Then, with precision, he makes the shot at hand, and skillfully directs the cue ball to a predetermined spot so it is poised for the next shot.

Salespeople who function at this skill level also carefully review the customer's needs, both stated and unstated, and skillfully sets in motion, a plan to address those needs either now, or at a later, more convenient date.

Objections rarely come up because the Counselor has taken the time to anticipate what objections may arise, and then build the answers to the potential objections into his or her presentation.

This salesperson will get every drop of business the customer has, not because of price, but because the customer knows the salesperson really cares about them, understands their needs, and will take the time to identify those needs and offer workable and credible solutions.

How Do Your Customers See You?

How do your customers see you? I mean, when the people you deal with regularly, your customers and prospects – when they view you as the person they do, or are considering doing business with, who do they see?

Are you someone they might classify as a "typical salesperson" – someone who is out to sell them another product or service, or who is interested more in the sale or commission they'll earn?

Or do your customers and prospects view you more as a counselor – someone they like and can relate to and who is genuinely interested in them, making sure they have the right product for their individual and specific needs, at the best possible price? And if what they've purchased does not, or will not work for them, or if they're not satisfied will be behind you making things right?

How you answer this basic and important question is critical to your success in business. It can mean the difference between enormous success, mediocrity, or even dismal failure.

And, it's a self-feeding mechanism. If you are viewed by your customers as a time waster or a product hustler, even if it is not stated, you will pick up that message yourself, and act reinforcing your customer's image of you.

If your customers welcome you as a counselor, or an advisor – someone with their best interests in mind – someone who can help them identify and solve their problems, they will feel good about you. And you will feel good about yourself, and the role you play relative to your customer. You will be and act more professional, more confident and can better help your customer with the solving of his or her needs and problems.

As you fill the role as a problem solver, you can't help but reinforce and strengthen that positive image in both you, and your customer's minds.

What Your Customers Really Want

As a businessperson, only 35% of the reason people buy the products or services you offer, is for the actual product or service itself.

The other 65% of the reason they buy, is for what you can do or provide for your customer beyond the product or service, and what that product or service does for the customer.

If you are trying to sell your customers and prospects *products and services*, you are wasting your time. They are only 35% interested in *products and services*.

But they are 65% interested in the benefits of *having you involved*.

Chances are good that your customers and prospects can buy the same product or service (or at least comparable ones) from any of several of your competitors.

And with that product or service, your competitor may offer several additional advantages.

They may have a lower price, better quality product, some added bonuses or extra services, a location that's more convenient, or a payment plan that fits their budget better.

In today's tough, competitive market, it's difficult to compete on price or product. You may command a certain advantage for a period time because you have a price lower than your competitors, but you and I both know that it will be short-lived, unless you're Wal-Mart.

You can never maintain a competitive position in the marketplace – long-term for any length of time because of the prices you charge or the products you provide.

It will be a matter of time before either one of your competitors lowers their prices or duplicates (or even betters) your product or you raise your prices because you no longer have the margins to justify your prices.

But there's one thing your customers can't get from any of your competitors. And that's you, and the empathy, the problem solving expertise and the knowledge, education and commitment to service you bring to his or her specific and unique situation.

Products and Services, or Advice?

So it is important to continually ask yourself (and be honest) the following question…

"How do your customers… the people who do business with you… your clients and prospects, see you?"

On the next page is an example of an easy method to find out.

Take a sheet of paper and draw a line down the middle.

On the left hand side at the top, label the column, "Products and Services."

Label the right hand column, "Help and Advice."

Every time you are in contact with a customer or prospect, whether they call you or you have a face-to-face meeting, evaluate the overall purpose of the meeting.

On the next page is a diagram demonstrating this simple process:

Products and Services	Help and Advice
⎪ ⎪ ⎪ ⎪ ⎪ ⎪ ⎪ ⎪ ⎪ ⎪ ⎪ ⎪ ⎪ ⎪	⎪ ⎪ ⎪ ⎪ ⎪ ⎪ ⎪ ⎪ ⎪ ⎪ ⎪ ⎪ ⎪ ⎪ ⎪ ⎪ ⎪ ⎪ ⎪ ⎪ ⎪ ⎪ ⎪ ⎪ ⎪ ⎪ ⎪ ⎪ ⎪ ⎪ ⎪ ⎪ ⎪ ⎪ ⎪ ⎪ ⎪ ⎪ ⎪

Did your customer or prospect look to you for the products or services you provide? Or did they seek your help, advice or counsel to help them decide what would solve a particular need or challenge they were encountering?

Once you've determined that, place a mark in the appropriate column. Then at the end of the month, evaluate the results of your list.

If you have more marks in the "Products and Services" column than in the "Help and Advice" column, you know what perception your customers have of you.

But equally important, you also know what you need to do to change that perception. You can then develop and implement a plan of action focusing on improving your image in the eyes of your customers. Then test yourself again several months later. By comparing your evaluation sheets over the period of a year or two, you can easily see the progress you're making.

Improvement is not always difficult. Often, a person may not know where they are weak or where they need to improve. But if you can isolate those areas that need improvement, you can then try to effect positive change.

"Live out of your imagination, not your history."

Stephen Covey

3

How Much Are You Worth?

Strategies for Determining and Increasing Your Value to Your Customers

You are in business for yourself. You may own your own business, or you may be associated with another company or firm, as either an employee, a partner or an independent contractor. Your working agreement or arrangement doesn't matter.

The important thing to realize is no matter what the arrangement or situation you find yourself in, you are working for yourself. If you work by commission the sales you make are not only putting dollars in your employer's pocket, they are putting dollars into your own pocket. The more you sell, the more you make.

Just consider yourself as a business that prospers or falters financially by the commission dollars you generate. The point is, even though you may work for, or associated with another company or concern, you are working for yourself to increase the money you earn for you.

Three Keys for Success

It's important to realize your success in whatever you do in business, or in life will always be determined by three things:

1. The need or demand for what you do,
2. Your ability to do it, and
3. The difficulty in replacing you.

How valuable are you and the service you perform, to other people?

To illustrate this point, let's apply our 3-step formula to the job of an elevator operator. In today's world of pushbutton, self-operated elevators, how much need is there for the job he or she performs?

Most people can operate an elevator themselves. It takes little knowledge or training, so an operator can be replaced with little difficulty. Elevator operators, if you can even find one, are not paid much.

Now, contrast the elevator operator and the money he or she commands with that of a professional major league baseball player. Specifically a player who's a good hitter.

What is the *need for what they do?* A look at attendance figures for baseball games will show more than just a few fans are interested in watching what they do. So the need is great.

How about the batter's *ability to do what he does?* Sports analysts say that the action of hitting a ball moving towards you at over 90 miles per hour is the single most difficult movement in sports.

In basketball, the target (the hoop) doesn't move. Same in golf.

While the ball moves, the hole, or goal, remains stationary. In football, there are 11 teammates all with a common goal of advancing the ball. But in baseball, it's the batter alone, trying to hit a small, 90 m.p.h. target with his bat. So it makes sense then, the more often a batter can hit the ball, the more he or she will be compensated.

Now, what about the *difficulty in replacing* a good batter? When only the best in the world can hit the target less than a third of the time, and most of the other players succeed far less than that, it doesn't take long to realize why the best hitters are among the highest moneymakers in the world.

Obtaining Superior Rewards

Now how about you? It's been said, you can tell how professional a person is by the size of their income at the end of the year.

And you can tell exactly how valuable the service you perform is, by how much people will pay you for it. If you do the same job everybody else does, and do it no better than the way they do it, you can't expect to earn more money, or be any more valuable than those other people. The market, by nature, will pay superior rewards only for superior goods and services. It will pay average rewards for average goods and services, and it will see that inferior rewards are paid for inferior goods and services.

You will be rewarded in direct proportion to the value you provide your customers. It's inescapable. That's the law of nature.

Now, if the products and services you sell or provide are similar in coverage and price to everyone else's (and most are, today), then the difference between you and other people in your position must be in the type and amount of personal service you provide your customers and clients.

This has to be the area you excel in – it becomes your competitive edge.

Guaranteeing Business Success

So one of the main keys to success in business is to make sure there is a great *need or demand for what you do.*

One of the best ways to guarantee is to only sell to qualified prospects. People who need, want and can pay for what you're selling. There may be people who need or want what you have, but if they can't afford to pay for it, or if you can't arrange suitable payment options for them, you'll spend a seemingly endless amount of time and get nowhere.

There may be people with the ability to pay, but not the need or want. In these cases, you can also waste considerable time, because surely, no sale will result from your efforts.

The second point is you are paid in direct proportion to your *ability to do what it is you do.* To identify, qualify and sell the products and services you offer to your prospects and customers, and then service their needs as they arise.

In some businesses, the sole function of salespeople is to seek qualified prospects and sell them the products or services offered by the business. The service work for the customer is provided by an office or support staff.

In other businesses, each salesperson is responsible in every way for each of their customer's needs, from the initial sale, to providing all the service the customer might require, including updating the product or service, customer complaints, changes of address, or any other service work that may be needed.

The determining factor then, is not your responsibilities, but how good you are at performing those responsibilities.

Third, remember, you are paid in direct proportion to the difficulty *in replacing you.*

When I think of this area, I think of Disneyland and

Disneyworld. They have little competition. And as far as theme parks? They are unsurpassed. Their average daily attendance figures bear this out.

Disneyland - California 35,342

Disneyworld, Epcot Center – Florida 78,082

Disneyland - Tokyo...........................32,877

With 146,193 guests visiting each day, and paying an average of $57 per person, the Disney properties are light years ahead of their nearest competition. And, why? Because they have met the criteria outlined in the 3-step formula.

Let's consider each of the steps of the formula as they apply to Disney.

First, is there a need for what they do? There must be. Entertainment is the largest and fastest growing business in the world today, both in terms of participants, and in total dollar revenue.

Next, how about Disney's ability to do what they do. With over 53 million people visiting their three parks each year, evidence would indicate they are doing at least a few things, if not a whole lot of things right.

And finally, the difficulty in replacing them? Nothing has come close yet, and with those 53 million people spending over $3 billion, odds are the people who visit the Disney properties are satisfied.

The Law of Unlimited Abundance

Walt Disney was a man of extraordinary vision and foresight. He knew what it would take to succeed in his chosen area of business, and he developed a formula that expressed his philosophy, and could be used in any business to ensure its success. He called it, his "Law of Unlimited Abundance."

Walt said it didn't matter what type of business or endeavor a person was engaged in, they could succeed and enjoy *unlimited abundance*, if they would simply follow his formula or plan.

Walt Disney's "Law of Unlimited Abundance," stated, that to succeed, you must,

"Do what you do so well, that the people who see you do it, will want to see you do it again, and will bring others to see you do it."

That's the credo that built the enormous successes of Disneyland and Disneyworld. And in their arena of operation, they stand alone.

Disney's Law Can Work For You!

It can be similar in your business world, too. The key is to, "*do what you do*," not what someone else does, but what *you* do. Don't copy. You simply do your job the way only you can. That's what makes you special, sets you apart from others, and attracts people to you.

Then you do what you do, "*so well*," that is, provide the service your customers require, want, or need in an exceptional manner. It leaves no room for mediocrity, it's "so well." Which implies exceptional performance.

And if you will do that so, "*the people who see you do it*," (your customers), "*will want to see you do it again*," (that's repeat business), "*and will bring others to see you do it*," (that's referral business), you too, can meet with an unparalleled success.

Because so few people perform in business that way, it sets you apart from all the competition. Customers can't get the service you offer from anyone or anywhere else. It's simply not available anywhere, at any price.

So, by default, you become unique, different, and difficult to replace. And it will be reflected in your business and your income. It has to. There's no choice. It is a basic, eternal law of nature. You simply reap the results of what you've sown.

You Reap What You Sow

The question you must answer in your mind is, "What are you going to sow, so you will reap the kinds of rewards you wish to have?"

In the world of business, this is a most critical question, and one you would do well to take the time to answer. Fact is, most business people simply don't understand how important the answer to this one question really is.

Many people go into business because it is something they have always wanted to do, or because they want a certain amount of freedom, or perhaps they want to be their own boss.

Now, those are not necessarily bad reasons, but they are selfish reasons mostly, and while they may sound good on the surface, in actuality, some may not be very practical.

If you go into business for selfish reasons, and fail to give the customer his or her rightful due, your chances of success are likely to meet with hard times.

Business, like farming, requires you do certain things in a particular order, if you are to realize an abundant harvest. Now the answer to the question,

"What are you going to sow, so you will reap the kinds of rewards you want?"

…is simple. You only have to look at the question backwards.

First, what kinds of rewards do you want? Second, what do you have to do to get those rewards? And third, who can give you those rewards?

If you will always remember, that although you may own or work for, or represent a certain company or organization, they are not who pays you.

The Customer Signs Your Paycheck

It really is the customer who signs your paycheck. And although see that your company's interests are always considered, you must not lose sight the customer is the boss.

They are the whole reason your job exists. They hire you to help them make good personal and business decisions. They trust you to help them see their problems or needs are solved or satisfied in an efficient and cost-effective manner, and they pay you well to do your job.

It is the wants, needs and desires of your customers that should determine all of your business activity. So the next logical step then, is to learn and understand just what your customer's wants, needs and desires are. And you find that out simply by interviewing and asking them. It is very important to listen carefully to what they say because sometimes there may be other, hidden or unstated wants or needs that may not be readily evident. And only by fully understanding their needs, can you be of meaningful service to them.

"Life is a series of problems. Do we want to moan about them or solve them?"

M. Scott Peck

4

Why People Buy

Identifying the Basic Motives That Make Your Customers Want To Buy

People don't buy for the sake of owning a certain product or service. Rather, they buy because of the benefits they receive as a result of owning that product or service.

The example traditionally used to illustrate this point, is that in one year, a quarter of a million quarter-inch drills were sold, and not one person who bought a drill wanted a quarter-inch drill. Instead, they bought the drills because they wanted the benefits the drill could provide... a hole.

People buy your products and services for the same reason... not for a hole... but for the benefits those products or services provides. Ask the next 10 prospects you meet if they want to buy the product or service you're selling, and chances are, you'll receive a negative answer.

Many factors influence people to react that way, and each person has his or her own reasons. Regardless of individual reasons, it's a fact, people don't want to buy *products*, and they often resent people trying to sell them.

People Buy for the Benefits

If you ask the same person that previously turned you down if they want the specific benefits the products or services you're selling will provide them, you will most likely receive a positive answer. They may give you a hard time about the prices you are charging, but usually the answer will be a "yes."

Like the quarter-inch drills, people are not interested in products, but they are interested in the benefits the products will provide them. It makes sense then, when making a presentation, you don't emphasize *products*.

Rather, talk in terms of *specific benefits,* and how those benefits apply directly to the particular prospect in front of you.

Each person is different, and each person has his or her own reasons for buying or not buying. And each person will buy for his or her own reasons – not yours or anyone else's.

If you try to sell them for any reason other than their own, you risk turning them off or otherwise alienating them, which usually destroys the sale you are trying to make, and any future sales.

Trying to figure out why people make certain decisions can be a complicated, even frustrating process. But an understanding of basic buying motives can make your job much easier.

Motives for Buying

Behavioral psychologists tell us seven basic motives move a person to action – causing them to buy. An understanding of these motives and how they apply to your customers and prospects when a buying decision is made, can give you a tremendous advantage.

1. Desire for Gain or Profit

Nobody likes to lose. People want something in return for their efforts and hard work. And the easier they can get it, the better. The success of the lottery games in various states bear testimony of people trying to find an easy way to get gain and profit.

The products you sell can help your customers realize their dreams for gain or profit, too. Your customers can and will invest in various types of products or services you sell – not to own them, per se, but to increase their profitability and the amount and value of their assets.

2. Fear of Loss, or Need For Security

People will go to great lengths to prevent losing something. To protect their property, some people install burglar or fire alarms, smoke detectors, or night-lights that automatically come on when movement is detected.

Some people carry spray cans of mace, or tear gas, while others have resorted to carrying guns or other weapons to protect their person.

Psychologists say the fear of loss or the need for security is perhaps, the greatest of all the motives.

If the products and services you sell can help protect your clients, their families or their businesses from loss, or if you can increase their security, either now or in the future, you owe it to them to capitalize on that fact as much and often .

3. Pride of Ownership, Or Status

People want to be noticed and recognized. Little boys ride bicycles with no hands, and little girls dress up, act out dance routines, and shout to their parents, "Watch me! Watch me!"

Adults do the same things, but in different ways. While they may not verbally shout out, they still say, "Watch me! Watch me!" just as loudly.

They do it by the cars they drive, the clothes and jewelry they wear, the houses they live in, and the material things they possess.

While people may buy because of the benefits, they like others to see the actual product. Sometimes it's just another way to say, "Watch me! Watch me!"

4. An Interest in Doing Something Easier or More Efficiently

We all want methods of doing things easier. One only must look around his or her home to notice the abundance of time and/or money-saving conveniences we all enjoy.

What about your products or services?

Do they somehow make a person's job, or a business' way of doing things easier or more efficient?

And if they do, what are the direct and indirect benefits to your prospect or customer?

Is this something you can capitalize on?

5. The Desire for Excitement or Pleasure

A popular bumper sticker states,

"He who dies with the most toys wins."

The message indicates people want excitement and pleasure. And it seems to suggest pleasure comes in the "having," rather than in the "getting." It's whoever has the most at the end that wins.

But in reality, "excitement" and "pleasure," for most people comes in the acquiring of things.

Think back about the times you have worked hard to get something, and how excited you were.

But then, once you had whatever it was you were working for, how the excitement dulled.

Sometimes it's not the end result that counts as much as acquiring.

A more practical interpretation of the bumper sticker might read,

"He who lives with the most toys wins!"

These applications must do with "things." Some people really enjoy acquiring "things," and even keep score by how much they accumulate.

Other people gain great pleasure or excitement knowing their family's future educational and livings needs, and retirement will be taken care of.

Business owners like to know their businesses are operating at peak efficiency and profitability, are meeting the needs of their customers, will be around for long time providing jobs and security for their employees and their families, and providing retirement funds for the owner when the business is sold.

6. Self Improvement or an Increase in Effectiveness

Your investment of both money and time in this book is a good example of your desire for self-improvement and increased effectiveness. People want and need to improve and to do things more efficiently.

Sometimes that involves taking risks with time or money. Not all risks must be "risky." Calculated risks based on well thought-out plans and outcomes are the safest way to go, and can contribute greatly to the successful improvement in effectiveness and efficiency.

7. The Desire for Importance or the Need to Feel Appreciated

According to noted psychiatrist, Dr. Abraham Maslow, this is one of the basic needs of all humans, acceptance and appreciation. Children want acceptance from their parents and peers, and parents want their children to remember them when they grow up and leave home.

In his book, *The Human Side of Enterprise,* Douglas McGregor explains that workers are motivated more by "significant works," and a feeling of being needed and appreciated, than by money.

People want to make a difference, and be appreciated for it. Fathers and mothers not only have an obligation to see their family's futures are provided for, but they want their family to understand and appreciate their efforts.

Business owners have an obligation to the people who buy from them, the employees who work for them, their employees' families, the suppliers and the vendors who sell to them. Too often, each of those groups of people live with an attitude of expectancy and entitlement. They expect the business owner will take care of them. How much better it would be if more appreciation would be shown to those who make our lives better.

If the products or services you provide the marketplace can help make this possible, you may have an open ticket to success because of the great-unsatisfied need that exists.

If you understand these basic motives and how they apply to your business of selling your products and services, and then sell to the needs (both stated and unstated) of your customers and prospects, you will prosper.

And if you are not prospering, it simply means you have not uncovered your prospect and customer's motives for buying. You are not addressing their specific needs. Usually you can't wait for your customers to tell you what they want. You have to be able to recognize their needs.

Remember, you are ultimately responsible for the success or failure of your business. If you are doing it right or wrong, either way, the marketplace will let you know.

The Loyalty of the Customer

Customers make an interesting study. It seems they always want the very most for the very least they must pay. They are ruthless, selfish, demanding and disloyal.

You know the story. You've done business with someone for several years and they've been good customers. You've given them the best service possible and you think they are your customers for life. But then some little thing possibly out of your control goes wrong, or they see an ad or get a call from a competitor, someone they've never met before, with a slightly lower price, and the next thing you know, they are gone, often without a single word to you.

At first, you don't notice it. But one day you realize it's been a while since you've seen or heard from that customer. When you find out what happened, you feel badly, because if they would have just called you, you might have been able to make a couple of changes and save the business. But it's too late, they're gone.

This scenario is repeated time and again with businesses owners from every company, who sell every type of product or service. It will happen. To pretend it doesn't, or won't happen, is simply deceiving yourself.

It's incredible how many business owners just write off losing a good customer. But that's not the thing you should do. Instead, now is the time to become even more proactive and go after the "lost" customer.

One of the best ways to minimize or cut down on the frequency of losing your good customers is to resell them on the reasons they bought from you. Regularly scheduled meetings or conversations with your customers to remind them of their motives can go a long way in helping insulate your business from the competition.

Remember, your competition has similar products, services and prices. Also, remember your customer's reasons for buying are only 35 percent based on those products, services, and prices. The other 65 percent is for what you can do for them.

Spend the time with them. Review their needs, wants and concerns. Remind them why they bought from you. Reinforce their motives, and their decisions for buying, and you will reduce your customer defection rate and develop not only loyal customers, but also friends.

"In every difficult situation is potential value. Believe this, then begin looking for it."

Norman Vincent Peale

5

The Main Purpose of Your Business

Getting and Keeping Customers…Profitability Is Priority Number One

When you have an effective system that will allow you to *profitably* get and keep *quality* customers that will return to do business with you over and over again, and then actively and enthusiastically refer you to others, your business will produce more profits than you might imagine. And then everything else falls into place.

If you don't have enough customers buying from you or using your services regularly, then you'll not likely stay in business for long, and will never have the chance to make a profit.

Now, let's take a minute and look closely at the individual components of this important business skill…

Knowing How to Profitably Attract Quality Customers

Customers are the lifeblood of any business. Without customers buying the products and services you offer, you wouldn't have a business to begin with. But customers alone aren't enough.

You want *quality* customers... customers who are pleasant to deal with. Customers who return to repurchase from you repeatedly. Customers who you can sell to and realize a reasonable profit from.

And you want to *profitably* attract them. The return you realize from your investment of advertising or marketing dollars to acquire new customers, should be positive. You want a positive ROI, or return on investment.

Next, you want to...

Ethically Exploit Their Maximum Financial Potential

Each of your customers has certain needs and wants. And the more of those needs and wants you can handle for them, the more benefits you can provide them, and the more profits you'll realize.

It should be your goal to sell as many products and services to your customers as they need.

You shouldn't take advantage of them or your relationship with them, but strive to sell them everything you can *ethically* justify selling them.

It really comes down to this, and I'll speak frankly. If you really provide the best products and services in the marketplace (if you don't, you'd better rethink your ethics and why you're in business), and if you really are the business who can serve your customers' needs better than anyone else (and if you're not, you either need to become that business or get out of the business), then you have a moral and an ethical responsibility to make sure every one of your customers at least takes advantage.

And do everything in your power *reasonable* and *ethical* to give them the opportunity.

Next, you want to…

Convert Your Customers to Advocates Who Actively and Enthusiastically Refer You to Others

By definition, an "advocate" is a backer, a supporter, a promoter, a believer, an activist, a campaigner, a sponsor.

The last thing you need is a database full of one-product, or one-service customers who buy the minimum amount from you, complain about your prices every time they make a purchase, and give the rest of their business to the company with the lowest prices or a "better deal."

There's no way you can make a profit on these types of customers. Besides, they make your life miserable and drive you crazy.

Who you want are customers who not only give you all (or the majority) of their business, but re-buy from you repeatedly, year after year. You want customers that are so happy and so pleased with what you do for them they actively and enthusiastically campaign for you. The story they tell about you so compels that the people they tell are nearly forced to call you and ask for your help. Those make your job fun, enjoyable and profitable.

And finally, you want to…

Keep Your Customers for Life

Reliable studies demonstrate the more needs a business handles for a customer; the longer they can expect that customer to do business with them.

In the insurance business for instance, an agent increases his chances of keeping an insured for three years or more by these percentages:

- 45% if the agent insures only the auto policies
- 50% if both the auto and homeowners policies are insured
- 60% with auto, homeowners and life policies, and
- **97% with auto, homeowners, life and health policies!**

While these figures are illustrative of the insurance business, the same principle is true of most other businesses. Banks, for instance, have studies that show the difference in customer retention with a customer that only has a checking account, versus another customer with multiple checking accounts, a savings account, an IRA, Safety Deposit box, their car financed through the bank, and several other services.

The idea is by serving all the needs your prospects or customers have, with the products and services you provide or have access to; you lock yourself in and the competition out.

And obviously, the longer you retain your customers, the more income you will earn from them, the more chances you will have to sell them additional products and services, and the more referrals you can get from them. It all adds up to increased profits for you.

Retention of your customers… the ones you've spent so much time, effort and money attracting and convincing to do business with you is critically important.

More than one study suggests it costs six times more to get a prospect to buy from you than it does to get an existing customer to purchase from you again, and it's sixteen times easier to sell an existing customer than it is a new prospect.

When you add it all up, for every 5% increase in customer retention, you'll generate a 30% to 45% increase in profitability over an 18-month period.

Depending on the products and services you sell, if your repurchase rate isn't in the high 90-percentile range, you have work to do.

A lost customer is more than just a lost customer, and their attending profits. It's much more. In future chapters, we'll be discussing how to determine what the actual cost of a lost customer is, and what to do to prevent them from leaving.

But for now, just keep this important point in mind... if you want to succeed in business, no matter what type of products or services you sell; you've got to have an intense focus on your customer. You've got to find out what they want and do everything you can to help them get it.

And if you want to make a fortune rather than just a living, you can't do it for only a few. You must do it for large numbers of people.

The success of your business will depend on how well you serve your customers... the people who buy from you!

"Our deeds determine us as much as we determine our deeds."

George Eliot

6

The Four Primary Ways to Grow Your Business

Maximizing the Return on Your Efforts in the Four Key and Critical Areas

The number one thing... and one of the most important things for any business owner, manager, entrepreneur or professional to realize, is there are four ways... four *principal* ways to grow a business – any business.

There are many tactics to grow your business, but for our discussion here, we'll be focusing on only the four primary ways to grow a business.

Other than some administrative functions, some of which are not under your direct influence or control, nearly everything you do to build or grow your business can be classified under one of four different and distinct areas, or categories, and if you learn this one simple concept and how to apply it, believe me, your competition won't stand a chance.

And the reason?

Because your competition not only doesn't understand this concept, most have never even heard of it.

Now, here's the first one of the four ways to grow your business. Simply...

Get More Customers

That's it. Build your customer base. Get more prospects to buy from you and become your customers.

You know how it works. When more people buy from you, you take in more gross dollars, and as a result (depending on your margins and overhead), you make more bottom line profits.

As a spin-off benefit, the more people you add to your customer base the larger it becomes, and the larger it becomes the more people you have to go back to for additional sales and the referrals they're capable of giving you.

It's in this one area where most business owners (including your competition, and probably, you, too, if you're honest), spend most of their time, effort and money.

If you've been in business for any length of time, you probably realize that getting new customers is not always the easiest, the most time-efficient, or most profitable thing you can do.

Most businesses only have one or two main methods of attracting new prospects to their businesses.

You probably know many businesses are heavy using telephone soliciting.

You, yourself, have probably gotten more than your fair share of calls, when you were just sitting down for dinner.

Chiropractors, car dealers, truck driving schools, and lawyers take a different approach. Many advertise heavily on television, especially during the afternoon hours to attract new customers. They've found a large part of their intended audience… the people who are most inclined to use their services, watch television during those hours, and it's a cost-effective way to reach them.

Each business, industry, or profession has their own methods and timing to contact those who are most likely to be interested in their products and services. What works for some businesses, may work for other businesses in the same or different industries or professions.

Think about your business and your company for a minute. Chances are, you, like nearly every other business owner in your industry or profession also utilizes one, or perhaps two main methods of attracting new prospects.

Most likely, the method you use is the same method nearly every other business uses. It's called the, *"That's how things are done in our industry or profession,"* method.

Typically, when a person first goes into business they look around and see what everyone else is doing.

Then they layout their office, shop or place of business just like every other similar type of business they've seen.

They look at what everyone else is doing to market or promote their businesses, products and services, and adopt those same marketing plans and methods to market or promote their business.

This activity isn't isolated to just a few businesses – nearly every business in nearly every industry or profession is guilty.

But, wait a minute. Who set up that system in the first place? And who says it's right, or that it's the best system for you to use? The fact is there are an unlimited number of methods of attracting new customers to your business, and your imagination is the only limiting factor.

Some of the best, most productive and cost-effective methods you can use, can be adapted from what others are doing in unrelated businesses.

Now, this brings up some questions. First, how observant are you? What are others who are in the same business you're in doing? And, how effective are they?

Next, look around at what other businesses... unrelated businesses in other, unrelated fields, industries or professions are doing. Have you seen what's working for them? Is there one business that just stands out, by doing something different or unusual? Or, do they all use the same marketing methods?

Next question: How creative are you? Can you look at what some of the other businesses are doing, and adapt (with a few minor changes), their methods to your business?

If you were brand new, just starting in business, and did not understand what anyone before you had done to attract new customers, what would you do? How would you get new customers? Would you use the same methods you use now, or would you do something different?

A dentist I consult with specializes in working with children and their teeth. He loves children. And he recognizes, as they get older, they may need braces, they'll probably get married, and have a spouse and children that will all need dental care.

So, he set up his reception room with a special, "kid-height" counter, so when the children come in, they can talk directly to the receptionist, transact their business just as an adult would, and schedule their next appointment. He's even decorated his reception area with artwork and pictures that some of his young patients have created.

How do you think those young people feel? Well, you probably guessed it. They absolutely love it there. And they tell their friends about it, too. And their parents? They're *thrilled*.

Imagine, having your kids *want* to go to the dentist! And then be treated, not like a second-class citizen, but as an equal, transacting business (with the parent's help), and having a hand in scheduling their future appointments.

What a learning and growing experience for them. And who do you think the parents use for their own dentist? That's right.

The spin-off business of catering to, and working with children, is their parents.

As the kids grow up and have families of their own, which dentist do you think they'll use… that they'll insist their spouse switches to, and they'll bring their own children to?

The relationship this dentist is building with those young people… of friendship, of trust and of caring, will provide him all the financial security he'll ever need, and allow him to do whatever he wants and go wherever he pleases for the rest of his life.

So, what about you and your business? What are you doing? Specifically, what marketing methods are you using, *right now* to attract new customers, and to build lasting relationships with them so they'll do business with you for a lifetime?

And second, how many marketing methods do you have working for you? There's a real danger in having just one or two main methods of attracting new customers.

One of my consulting clients depended almost entirely on a telemarketing team to acquire leads for their salespeople to follow up with. When a well-funded competitor opened for business not far away, they hired nearly all that business' telemarketing staff, and nearly shut the business down. The business was nearly a total disaster.

When they called me in as a consultant, I could see we had to do something quick, just to save the business. So, we got to work and hired and trained a whole new telemarketing crew, and got the business up and running again.

But then we looked at other marketing options and put together an effective direct-mail program, started a proactive referral-generating system, and worked out some joint ventures and host-beneficiary relationships with other, complementary, but noncompeting businesses.

Now, if something happens to any of their marketing methods, they have other strategies or other "pillars" in place that can keep the business from collapsing, and keep it running smoothly.

What about your business? How can you apply this?

Well, why not start by going back and revisiting the questions I asked earlier. Then see if there are areas you need to improve in.

Make sure you're not dependent on only one or two main methods of attracting new customers.

New customers are important to your business, there's no question. They're vital... not only to the growth of your business, but to the very survival of the business.

It's critical you have multiple systems in place to ensure your business continues running, *and growing*, uninterrupted, if anything unexpected happens.

Because of the limited space in these pages, we can't talk about all the methods of getting new customers, but in the training materials and workshops we conduct, we go into great detail on effective ways to attract prospects by the bushel, and convert them into loyal, long-term customers. See the Market Ownership Group Website at marketownershipgroup.com for more info.

As important as getting more new customers are, there are still three more methods to grow your business. And each of these methods is more profitable, more effective, and gives you greater potential for leverage than the first method.

Let's talk about number two…

Get Your Customers to Make Larger Average Purchases

Increase the average transactional value of their purchases. Or more simply, get them to spend more money when they buy something from you.

This is the quickest and easiest way there is to increase your profits. One thing that continually amazes me is the number of businesses with extensive and expensive plans in place to acquire more customers.

Yet, very few have paid much attention to this highly profitable, and easily leveraged step of increasing the size of the order... getting more money from each of your customers every time they buy from you.

If you think for a minute about how easy this is and how profitable it can be, you'll see why it's such a powerful concept. And, you'll also see why nearly every fast-food restaurant has embraced, has mastered, and requires every person who takes orders, understands, and is proficient in using the "up-sell" and "cross-selling" principles.

Think back about your own fast-food restaurant experience. You drive up to the speaker and place your order... a sandwich and a drink. And then what happens? A voice comes back over the speaker and asks if you'd like an apple pie, or fries with your order. At least it used to be that way.

That's an example of cross-selling. Selling an additional product besides, or beyond the initial purchase.

Or, they used to suggest you "super-size" or "giant-size" your order. That's an example of an up-sell... increasing the size of the initial order.

If you take them up on their suggestion, what they've done is just increase their profits *substantially*, since they made an additional sale, but had no acquisition or marketing costs.

They realize, a certain percentage of their customers will say, "Yes." And the only reason they say, "Yes," is because a suggestion was made to them. So they play the numbers game.

And the result? Well, by being aware of what their customers might want, but not ask for on their own, and then by asking questions or making suggestions, they bring in a substantial number of dollars. And other than the actual cost of the product, those dollars are pure profit.

Here's another technique fast food restaurants frequently use. It's called "bundling," or "packaging."

It's where they combine a sandwich, a drink and fries, then throw in a couple of "bonus" items, like maybe a cookie and a toy. They put it all together in one package, and give it a name like, "Happy Meal."

They'll charge you less for the package than what each of those items purchased separately would have cost, but the total dollar amount you spend will be higher.

And, since there were no marketing costs involved, other than the cost of the items, themselves, it's pure profit, and it goes straight to their bottom line.

Now, what does that have to do with you, and your business?

Well, you may not be in the fast food business, but the same principles can still apply. Just ask yourself this question: "What additional products or services do you have that would be natural complements to what your customers initially buy from you?"

Well, you know the answer to that and I won't go into all the details here. But for instance, if you have the type of business that offers more than one product to your customers you have a tremendous advantage to capitalize on the up-selling, cross-selling and bundling techniques.

Some types of businesses, such as insurance companies that may offer only one product or service can also benefit from these strategies by packaging certain policies that cover multiple family members, adding riders, or including other complementary services that go beyond the actual policies themselves.

Do these things seem like common sense to you? Well, they probably do. But as I mentioned before, it's surprising how few businesses make effective use of these three simple principles.

Think about it. In reality, you have an obligation to your customers… the people who trust you to provide them good quality products and services, give them sound advice and who hand over their hard-earned money to you… to make sure they get the best value, the best use and the most enjoyment from their original purchase.

And if you have additional items, either products or services, that can enhance their value, their use or their enjoyment, then your obligation is to do everything that's reasonable and ethical, to see they at least take advantage of those items.

Again, it's playing the numbers game. Some will take advantage of your offer, and some won't. But at least, you will have given them the opportunity, and you will have fulfilled your obligation to them.

You haven't decided for them. You've given them a choice, and you've let them decide.

If you come across as sincere, they'll not see you as being pushy, but they'll realize you are trying to do them a favor… to help them get more value, more use, and more benefit from their decision and their purchase.

And they'll come back to do business with you again, and again, and will refer others to you.

Up-selling, cross-selling and bundling… these are only three of more than a dozen immediate, profit-producing methods to skyrocket your business to the next level.

If you do nothing more than incorporate these three techniques in your business (which you should be able to do within the next twenty-four hours), you'll blast your profits through the roof.

Think about it… increasing your sales… increasing your *profits*… without increasing your expenses. It's an exciting concept, and it can add an *immediate* twenty, thirty, even forty percent or more, *in pure profits* to your bottom line!

Now, let's move on to the third way to grow your business…

Get Your Customers to Buy From You More Often

Increase the frequency of their purchases. Get them to come back, Give them reasons to *want* to come back and to continue doing business with you. The longer your customers go between purchases from you, the more chance they have of buying from your competition.

It's like, "Out of sight, out of mind." You need to constantly stay in front of your customers with educational information, and notices of changes in the law or updates regarding the products or services they've purchased from you that can affect them. And you need to tell them about new products, new lines, special incentives and other offers that might benefit them.

The idea is two-fold: One, to "lock" your customers in, so they can't afford to do business with anyone else, and second, to make it so attractive to do business with you, they wouldn't even consider going anywhere else.

What you really want to do, is lead your customers to the inescapable and undeniable conclusion, they would have to be out of their minds to even consider doing business with anyone else but you, regardless of the selection of products or services you provide, the prices you charge, your location, or the relationship they may have with the organization they're doing business with.

Let me give you some real life examples of how this works: One of the clients I consult with owns a restaurant. And for his business customers who like to take their clients to lunch, he offers some lunches for a pre-paid, discounted price.

By doing this, he "locks in" his customer, gets his money up-front, and makes it convenient for everyone. The customer simply signs the check, which includes the tip. No money changes hands during or after the lunch, and new customers are constantly being introduced to his restaurant. Many of those new customers take advantage of the same arrangement for their clients.

Here's another example. A car wash offers a special pre-paid, discounted card that's good for some car washes. It's a great deal for people because you save money and when the card is filled, you have a free wax job coming. It's a good deal for the car wash too, because they've gotten their money up front, and have locked the customer away from the competition.

Here's one more. The store my wife buys shoes from offers "points" program. Every so often, she receives a notice in the mail informing her of how often she's accumulated. Now, she may not have been to the store for quite a while, but when she gets that notice and sees the credit she has coming, she nearly always makes it back to the store within a couple of days. And she hardly ever leaves empty handed.

Airlines offer upgrades and mileage bonuses for those who fly with them regularly. And countless other businesses offer similar programs.

Now, let's apply this concept to you and your business. What can you think of that you could do, that will endear your customers to you? To lock them in, and get them coming back more often and even refer others to do business with you.

Do you have an educational newsletter or special informative reports you periodically send them to keep them updated?

Do you send postcards, or do you have a website that keeps them informed of new items and promotions?

Do you hold special "Customer Appreciation Sales" or events?

How about a frequent buyer club for your more loyal customers?

What about a Referral Reward system that recognizes or compensates your customers for referring their friends?

Let your customers know you value them, appreciate them, want them to come back, and to make doing business with you fun, risk-free, rewarding, and easy.

I'm sure you can see the ideas are unlimited. And while the restaurant, car wash and shoe store examples may not apply directly to your business, I've included them to serve as a stimulus so you can think of what you might apply in your business that can help you develop trust and loyalty with your customers.

In our coaching programs, we go into great detail, and discuss over two-dozen very specific strategies that create an almost magnetic effect, that keeps your customers returning time and time again.

We lead you by the hand and help you develop personalized and effective strategies that keep them saying, "I'll be back"... strategies that keep them "insulated" from, and locked out of your competition. To learn more check out the Market Ownership Group website at marketownershipgroup.com.

Now let's talk about the fourth method to grow your business. And that is, to...

Extend Your Customers' "Average Buying Lifetime"

We call that, "Customer Retention."

Here's what I mean: How long, on average, do the people who buy from you, your customers, remain your customers?

How long do they continue doing business with you before they move on? Are they one-time buyers? Do they stay with you for a year, five years or ten years? Have you ever stopped to figure it out? This is an important step, and one we'll be discussing in more detail in later pages.

Next, what are you doing in your business to make sure your customers *continue* doing business with you? If you have no strategic plan, a *working system* in place, you will lose a certain percent of your current customers to the competition.

There's no question about it. Your competition... *right now*...

*right this very minut*e is making plans and trying to take your customers away from you.

The question for you is not, "What are you going to do about it?"

The *real* question is, "What are you *currently* doing about it?"

"What are you doing about it *right no*w?"

What plans… what *systems* do you have in place to keep your customers from defecting to the competition?

Let's talk about your customers for a minute. Are they *thrilled* enough with the products you offer and the services they receive from you to continue doing business with you year after year?

What if you answered "yes" to that question?

My next questions would be, "Are you sure?"

"How do you know?"

"Where did you get your information?"

"How reliable is it?"

"Can you explain in detail, the *system* you have in place for finding out?"

Notice I said, "Are they *thrilled* enough?" Not "are they *satisfied* enough?" There's a big difference between being *thrilled* and being *satisfie*d.

Last year, over 200 million Americans stopped doing business with companies they were "satisfied" with. And sixty percent of so-called "satisfied" customers switch companies or brands regularly.

As a business owner, you can't afford not to thrill your customers, or to build trust in you and your business. The cost is too high, and unfortunately, most business owners simply don't understand it. Let's look at what the potential cost could be to you if you fail to do these things:

Let's say you make $200 in sales per year from your average customer.

And let's say for many reasons, 100 customers stop doing business with you each year. They may die or move away. They may no longer have need for your products or services; they may switch companies, have a relative in the business, or possibly have a bad experience with someone in your company.

Or, they may just simply disagree with some policy or procedure. It could be a falling out with a staff member or employee, a personality conflict, miscommunication, a problem they had with one of your products, or perhaps a feeling of neglect from you or someone in your business. It really doesn't matter what the reason, they just stop doing business with you.

Well, those 100 customers no longer paying you $200 this year just cost you $20,000. But, that's not all. What if those 100 customers tell five others about their experience with you?

That's an additional 500 potential customers who won't be doing business with you this year (or maybe ever).

And if each spent an average of $200, that's $100,000 you won't be receiving from them, *PLUS* the $20,000 you lost on your existing customers who left.

That brings the total in lost income to *$120,000 in just one year!*

It's not unusual for some businesses to bring in a hundred (or more) new customers each month. That's twelve hundred-plus, customers a year. And they end up only netting a 150 or 200 increase at year-end (sometimes not even that).

Well, what happened to the other over 1,000 customers? Where did they go? Surely, they all didn't die, or move away.

But, you know, most business owners don't concern themselves with what, or whom they've lost. They just focus on their net gain. They figure if they finish the year with more customers or more sales than they started with, they're ahead.

Now, let's suppose you gave those 100 lost customers reasons… good, compelling, life or business enhancing reasons to continue doing business with you this year.

And let's suppose each told those same five people about their now-positive experience with you.

Well, there's $20,000 you wouldn't have lost in the first place, and another $100,000 you might pick up from their referrals or by their word of mouth.

The point is, customers are important – *all* customers. They're critical. There's no question about it. You and I both know a business can't remain in business, unless it has someone to buy its products and services.

Those "someone's" are people. Real people. People like you and me. If you sell your products to the business community, remember, businesses don't buy from businesses.

People in business buy from other people in business. It's people you market to. Not businesses.

Here's an interesting point: Most business owners know exactly how much they have tied up in furniture, fixtures and equipment. They can tell you, nearly to the penny, how much each item costs, how old it is, how much it's depreciated and what the remaining life expectancy is.

That's important information for any business to have. There's no question about it. But what's amazing are very few business owners know what the value of their most important asset is… their customers.

Think about how this whole concept relates to your business, for a minute. What is it you can do, *specifically*, to extend your customer's buying lifetime with you? Why not take a few minutes and answer these questions?

First, who are your customers … those buying from you now?

Who are their family members?

Do you know the names and ages of their spouse or children?

Do you know where they work?

What about their spouse or children?

What are their hobbies or interests?

Do you know why they purchased a certain product or service?

Do you know who their friends, neighbors or relatives are?

What about your staff or employees? Do you know how they treat or feel about your customers?

Do they, or do you have *favorite* customers? What makes them a "favorite?" Is it how much they spend? How often they come in? Their personality? And how do you treat those customers? Any different from the others?

Do you have regular staff meetings and talk about how to think like a customer?

What you would want if you were a prospect considering doing business with you for the first time? Or maybe an existing customer considering giving repeat business to your establishment or organization?

Or, perhaps considering referring a friend, a family member or an acquaintance?

Do you have a training system in place to teach your staff how to handle or deal with difficult customers? Short-tempered customers? Analytical customers?

Do you have a plan for moving people up the "Loyalty Ladder?" From Suspect to Prospect to Shopper. Then on to Customer, Client, and Advocate. And, finally to convert them into Raving Fans?

When a customer stops doing business with you, do you know why? Do you have a *system* in place to find out?

What would you have to do differently to get your customers to buy from you for, say, 5 ½ years, instead of just 5 years?

Believe me, if you will take the time to go through these questions and formulate answers for them, and then incorporate the information into your business practices, you can work wonders towards extending the buying lifetime of your customers. And you'll add *significant* profits to your bottom line.

We've covered a lot of ground and many ideas. So, let's pause for a minute, and recap what we've discussed up to this point. There are four primary ways grow a business.

First, **get more customers**. And as I mentioned, this is a vital step. But it's also the most difficult and the most costly.

Second, get **your customers to spend more money with yo**u… increase the average transactional value of each sale. And remember, this is the fastest and the easiest way to add immediate profits to your bottom line.

Third, **get your customers coming back to buy from you more ofte**n.

And, fourth, **extend your customers' buying lifetime**. Retain them, keep them as customers and get them coming back if you can. It's simple. Nearly everything you do to build and grow your business can be slotted under one of these four categories. As I mentioned earlier, there are over two-dozen ways to apply these concepts and build your business, but for now, if you'll work on these four primary methods, you'll absolutely run circles around your competitors.

As you take a good, close-up look at these four areas, you'll see it really boils down to effectively marketing your business to your customers and potential customers.

The success of your business enterprise depends, largely, on how effective your marketing system is.

And that means if you want your business to excel… to really excel… if you want to virtually eliminate your competition, and become the dominating force in your marketplace, then you've got to think of yourself as being in the *marketing* business, not in the product or service selling business.

You need to consider yourself as the head of a marketing organization that sells the products and services your business offers.

Once you operate effectively, you'll find your job becomes much easier and much more enjoyable, and your prospects and customers will seek you out and referring others to you, rather than you chasing after them. The net result will be your marketing costs will plummet, and your profits will skyrocket!

"Only a life lived for others is a life worthwhile."

Albert Einstein

7

How Much Are Your Customers Really Worth?

Determining the Lifetime Profit Value of Your Customers

There's little debate about this: Your existing customers or clients are your most valuable assets. The question is, how much are they worth?

How much money... how much *profit* will you realize from each of your customers, over their "buying lifetime" with you?

This is such an important concept, and I can't say it strongly enough, that just knowing and understanding this one thing, can have a bigger impact on your business than just about anything else you can do.

Once you understand it, a whole new set of factors will come into play, and can absolutely revolutionize the way you look at your business, the way you *do* business, and the profits you'll generate. Let me give you an example to explain.

Let's say your average sale is $50. And let's say your average customer buys from you four times per year.

So from those four transactions, you realize $200 in income. And let's say this customer does business with you on average, for 10 years. Over that 10-year period (or their "lifetime" of doing business with you), this customer has been worth $2,000 in income to you.

Now, let's expand this example to a theoretical base of 1,000 customers and see what it means. Those 1,000 customers at $200 a year nets you an annual income of $200,000.

Let's assume with the proper programs in place, you're able to increase each of the four ways to grow your business we discussed earlier, by only 10 percent. Here's what happens:

First, the number of customers you have increases from 1,000 to 1,100.

Next, the average transaction amount per sale increases from $50 to $55.

Third, the average number of purchases per customer increases from four times 4.4 times.

So, the annual income from your customer base will increase from $200,000 ($50 x 4 transactions x 1,000 customers) to $266,200 ($55 x 4.4 x 1,100 customers). That's an increase of $66,200 a year!

A huge increase!

But if you think that's exciting, wait until you see what happens if you extended your customer's buying lifetime by just 10 percent.

Let's say your customers stay with you for 10 years, on average. Your lifetime value from those customers over that period of time would normally be $2,000,000. But, if you can extend that 10 years by just 10 percent to 11 years, your total dollar value from these customers will increase from $2,000,000 to $2,928,200 ($266,200 x 11 years)!

An increase of $928,200... nearly a million dollars! That's a *major* increase!

But that's not all. Let's say you put an effective referral generating system in place, and just 10 percent of your 1,000 customers send you a referral with a buying profile the same as your average customer.

That's an additional 100 customers who will bring you income of another $266,200 over the 11 years ($55 x 4.4 renewals x 100 customers x 11 years).

Total it all up, and you just made an additional $1,194,400! That's an average of $1,085,818 per year over the 11 years! Sound impossible? Well, it's not. And it's not all that difficult, either. It can be done by simply increasing each of the four areas by only 10 percent!

Now, how hard would that be to do in your business? Could you realistically, and with some help, increase each of the four areas we discussed, by ten percent? What about twenty percent?

Some businesses I consult with, after realizing the power of this key concept, and the others we've discussed, have increased their businesses by as much as a hundred percent, or more in less than a year.

Maybe the numbers and figures I've discussed are realistic for you and your business, and maybe they're not. And maybe you can't increase each area by the same percentage. That's okay. It doesn't matter.

The point is you probably have room for improvement in one, or more of the four areas. And if you want your business to be a viable force in the marketplace, to give you the lifestyle, the satisfaction and the income you want, you will have to take some proactive steps.

Knowing the Value of Your Customers Influences the Way You Treat Them

As I mentioned before, just knowing how much your customers are worth to you can be invaluable, and can help you in several ways.

First, we know people don't do business with the same company or business forever. They stop doing business or change whom they do business with for many reasons, and we've already discussed some of those.

But, if you just know, for instance, that your typical customer stays with you for say, ten years, on average, they're not just a one or two-time sale, you may treat them differently.

You may treat them with more respect, more kindness, and more courtesy. You may give them special treatment. And you may even invite them to special, invitation-only, preferred customer seminars or events.

Once you see your customers in a different light, you may do things differently to get them to stay longer as customers.

Next, if you know what the Lifetime Profit Value of your customers is, you'll probably discover you can spend far more to acquire a new customer than you originally thought.

If your average customer is worth $2,000 in income to you, you can, theoretically, afford to spend up to $2,000 to bring in a new customer and still break even.

In theory, you could spend that $2,000 and still make a profit on the other "back end" products you might sell them.

And, if you put an effective referral-generating program in place, you can spend that same $2,000, and make your profits on the referrals they generate.

You and I both know it's unrealistic to think you can really afford to spend your full lifetime income ($2,000), to get each new customer. And I'm not suggesting that.

In reality, you *can't* spend the entire $2,000. You have to be concerned about things like overhead, cash-flow and reserves. You can't spend money you don't have.

And, make sure the customers you attract, at least match the profile of your average customers, or perhaps are even a little better than average.

There are several other things you need to be aware of, such as, "Cost of Acquisition," "Cost of Retention," understanding your margins, and calculating the Marginal Net Worth of your customers.

Unfortunately, we don't have time to cover them in sufficient detail, here.

Knowing the Value of Your Customers Influences How Much You Can Spend To Get a New One, or Keep an Existing One

What it really comes down to, are two questions: How much can you *afford* to spend, and how much are you *willing* to spend to attract new business?

You may find you can, and will spend five or six times what your competitors spend. And if they're not willing to keep up with you, your business may just explode and leave them in the dust.

Just knowing your *margins* and you could, if you had to, spend up to that $2,000 amount and still break even, gives you a *tremendous* edge over your competition.

Here's a real-life example: My wife and I have a favorite restaurant we like to go to about twice a month. And our meals typically come to about $30. So $30 times 24 meals adds up to $720 in gross sales for the year.

Let's suppose we continue to patronize the restaurant for, say, 10 years. That's our buying lifetime with this restaurant. That gives the restaurant $7,200 in sales.

If over that 10-year period, we refer 10 people, five of whom become regular customers (and that's not very many in 10 years), with spending patterns similar to ours, they'll spend an additional $36,000. (That's five people, times $7,200 a year.)

Add that to the $7,200 we spent, and we've handled generating $43,200 for the restaurant. Even after deducting expenses for overhead, salaries and food costs, the restaurant still realizes a substantial number of profit dollars from the efforts of just one couple.

Restaurant Example

A. Amount of average sale	$ 30
B. No. of sales/year/customer (2 x per month)	24
C. Gross income per year per customer (A x B)	$ 720
D. No. of years customer patronizes restaurant	10
E. Gross income over buying lifetime (C x D)	$ 7,200
F. No. of referrals from customer over buying lifetime	10
G. % of referrals who become a customer	50 %
H. Referrals who become customers (D x E)	5
I. Gross income from referrals (E x H)	$ 6,000
J. Total value of a loyal customer (E + I)	$ 13,200

Now, here's a question: Could that restaurant afford to give away a free meal to attract a new customer? Remember two of us are spending $30, so one meal costs $15, and out of that, about a third of it (or, maybe $5) is profit.

So, the meal only costs the restaurant $10 for the two meals, and only part of that $10 goes to cover the cost of the food.

The rest of the expense is in overhead, which would have to be paid whether a meal was served.

The answer is yes, they *can* afford to give away a free meal. Not only that, they can afford to do several things to not only attract new customers, but more important, make their existing customers feel more appreciated and more special. And you know, when someone feels noticed and important, appreciated and special, it's just natural they'll want to return.

Let's imagine, for a minute, you are a long-time, faithful customer of a certain restaurant. And you brought your family, your clients or your business associates with you to eat there regularly.

How would *you* feel, if sometime, the manager of the restaurant were to offer you and your party a free dessert as a special appreciation gift for your loyalty and for the extra business you brought them? Would a little display of appreciation cause you to want to return again? I think it's safe to say it probably would.

And what about the people with you? How would they feel? Would they want to go back to that restaurant? Sure they would. What would the restaurant's hard costs of those desserts be? Would the restaurant lose any money on that gesture?

Well, it's not likely. Once you know how much profit your customers are worth to you, long term, only then can you determine how much you can afford to give away, or to spend, to get new customers, or to keep your existing customers coming back. And you can experiment with different offers to see which ones work best.

Now, here's another thought. Let's say the owner of the restaurant runs an ad, or does a mailing to attract new customers.

And let's say he spends $1,000 for the ad or the mailing, and two couples come in for dinner, and each spends $30.

Well, he's taken in $60. But the ad costs were $1,000. So what does he do? What would his competition do?

Does he consider the ad or mail campaign a loser… a total bust… and stop running it? That's what most business people do.

But what about you? What would you do? Well, if you understand the concept of Lifetime Profit Value and Marginal Net Worth, you'll probably think differently.

When you consider the Lifetime Value of those customers and realize with the proper care and attention those customers could handle $43,200 each, or $86,400 for the two, it changes the picture.

Those numbers are gross revenue figures, and you have to deduct for expenses. And it's over a 10-year period. But, still, that represents significant money. And all from a $1,000 ad. An ad most business owners would have given up on.

Now, I'm not saying you have to settle for, and be happy with low response rates for your ads. You don't. Always try to improve your ads, your letters, your offers… and give good, compelling reasons and benefits for someone to do business with you.

That's an entire subject, itself, and one we don't have time to discuss in great detail here. But one we take seriously, and spend considerable time on in our online workshops and coaching programs. For more info, check us out at marketownershipgroup.com

Let's go back and think about our restaurant example for a minute. Did this idea of stopping an ad just because it didn't break even, or produce a profit for you sound unusual? Different? Strange? Well, maybe to some people, in some businesses.

But, supermarkets and department stores use their own adaptation of this technique all the time. You've probably heard it referred to as a "loss leader."

What they do, is advertise a few products at, or below cost to bring new customers in to their store, knowing the customer will usually buy more products once they're in the store.

And also knowing, unless they get someone to visit their store in the first place, they could never stand a chance of making additional or repeat sales, or getting referrals from them. And additional and repeat sales to existing customers are easier to make, and usually always bring higher profit margins.

Just remember this important point:

The first sale means nothing… unless you're planning on going out of business next week.

You have to consider the Lifetime Profit Value…what your customer is worth to you, if you really want to succeed.

How can you apply this concept of Lifetime Profit Value in your business?

Well, the first thing you can do is determine what your average income per sale is. The Lifetime Profit Value Calculator below is provided for you to use in calculating the Lifetime Profit Value of \your own customers. Fill out with your current figures to get an idea of how much your customers are worth to you.

The LPV of Your Customers (Actual)

A. Amount of average sale	$
B. No. of sales/year/customer (2 x per month)	
C. Gross income per year per customer (A x B)	$
D. No. of years customer patronizes restaurant	
E. Gross income over buying lifetime (C x D)	$
F. No. of referrals from customer over buying lifetime	
G. % of referrals who become a customer	%
H. Referrals who become customers (D x E)	

I. Gross income from referrals (E x H)	$
J. Total value of a loyal customer (E + I)	$

The calculator below is provided so you can calculate what kind of a difference it will make to your business if you increased each area by 10 percent.

Remember as you do these calculations, this is a very simplified calculation. In our consulting sessions, we get very detailed and consider many more areas. So the results you'll see in actuality will be dramatically increased. But for a simple and easy to demonstrate way to determine your customers' value to you, these basic calculators will do nicely.

The LPV of Your Customers (+10%)

A. Amount of average sale	$
B. No. of sales/year/customer (2 x per month)	
C. Gross income per year per customer (A x B)	$
D. No. of years customer patronizes restaurant	
E. Gross income over buying lifetime (C x D)	$
F. No. of referrals from customer over buying lifetime	
G. % of referrals who become a customer	%
H. Referrals who become customers (D x E)	
I. Gross income from referrals (E x H)	$
J. Total value of a loyal customer (E + I)	$

"Differentiate or Die."

Al Reis & Jack Trout

8

How to Create Your Unique Selling Proposition (USP)

Answering the Question of Why Should I Buy From You?

If you are struggling with marketing your business, perhaps what you're missing is an effective Unique Selling Proposition (USP). Your USP is a precise statement of why your business is special. It MUST differentiate you from your competitors. Your USP should state at least one unique benefit your customer will receive. It must be specific, concise and meaningful. The following are tips on how to understand and develop your very own effective USP.

According to well known marketing guru, Dan Kennedy, *[who has been featured repeatedly in SUCCESS MAGAZINE, in USA TODAY, in INC., and in countless newspapers, syndicated columns, trade journals]*, your Unique Selling Proposition (USP) must answer the following question:

"Why should I do business with you above any and all other options, including doing nothing, or whatever I'm doing right now?"

If your answer to the above question is vague or general, you will have trouble convincing people to do business with you. Your USP must **instantly** tell people why they should do business with you above all other choices. Your answer must also be specific, concise, and meaningful.

Here's an example of an effective USP that Dan Kennedy used at a recent conference I attended. Dan spoke about a well-known company - the biggest in their field - in an extremely competitive industry. **This company became the biggest in their field entirely because of their USP.** The company Dan spoke about is Domino's Pizza. Consider Domino's USP:

"Fresh, hot pizza delivered to your door in 30 minutes or less, guaranteed!"

This USP built Domino's into a pizza empire! Too bad, they stopped using it.

Let's look at what made Domino's USP successful?

First, it specifically answers the question of why should I do business with them. The answer is, call them if I want *fresh, hot pizza delivered to my door in 30 minutes, guaranteed.*

Second, this USP is very specific and meaningful. It doesn't say, "it'll be there soon." Or, "it will be delicious." It says only that you will get fresh, hot pizza delivered in **30 minutes**, guaranteed!

You can imitate Domino's Pizza USP to create a USP for your own business. You just need to think about how your business answers the question listed above.

Another aspect of an effective USP is that when you tell someone your USP, it should prompt this response:

"Really? How do you do that?"

Say you're at a party and someone asks you what you do. Instead of telling them your title or what you do, tell them your USP. If you tell them, "I'm an automotive recycler," that person will merely nod and smile.

. . . let's say your USP is:

"I save business owners thousands of dollars each year by _____."

Or...

"I give _____ that shows any business how they are almost always blowing thousands of dollars a year on _____."

Or...

"I am a _____expert who shows companies how to add extra profits to their bottom line by teaching them how to save money on their _____ costs."

Or...

"In 15 minutes, I show people how to save hundreds, even thousands of dollars on _____ they regularly overpay for."

Or... "I show businesses who spend $x,xxx a year on _____ how to protect themselves from being overcharged."

With these USPs, there's a good chance a prospect will ask you, "Really, how do you do that?" You then tell them about how your business can save them money.

How To Develop Your USP

The first real secret to developing your Unique Selling Proposition is to first develop the unique positioning of your business, or the unique strategic position. This is the overall unique position you occupy in the public's mind. What is your company's dominance? What makes you special to your customers or prospects? If you occupy no position in the public's mind, then you have a marketing problem.

A strategic position statement is something like a mission statement for your company. You want this statement to explain how you view your company and how you view it within the rest of your marketplace.

Nordstrom's is a good example of strategic positioning. It's a department store making excellent profit margins while their competition is going out of business. They've taken a unique strategic position; they're number one in service that goes all the way back to their USP . . . *Service Above And Beyond All That Is Expected."*

It's impossible to be the best in all categories and that's why you need to figure out what makes your company unique and what your strategic positioning will be. What's your number one calling card or claim to fame going to be? There has been tons written on the subject, "positioning". If you're not familiar with this concept, then you should read the book, *"Positioning, The Battle For Your Mind"* by Al Ries and Jack Trout. Positioning has been THE marketing philosophy for most successful companies over the last ten years.

But what is "positioning" and how can you use it? Some examples:

APPLE has been first at innovation. They want to be first in whatever's next in technology.

Wal-Mart is the cheapest store, they won't be undersold. Low price and full lines are their battlefields for your mind.

"What's the best battlefield (Strategic Position) for you to take?"

Understand that any decision to buy from, or use a company's services, first takes place in the mind of the customer. If you're company, products, or services are not in their mind, they probably won't use you. **You basically, "aren't there" without a position.**

Some of the most common examples of positioning are service, speed of delivery, latest technologies, guarantees, and lowest price.

Your company has probably already carved out a niche for itself. But, if you're like most business owners, you probably haven't identified your niche. Usually it's the salespeople and customers who know the niche better than the owners do.

When it comes down to it, customers really know a company's niche best. You can use the 80/20 rule to research about your company. The 80/20 rule is that 80% of a company's profit comes from 20% of their customers. Find out who the "20%" of your best customers are. Find out why they are doing business with you instead of someone else. This will tell you where your **real niche** or **core competency** is. If you think you do one thing and your best customers think you do another thing, you need to decide. What causes this difference in perception? Did your marketing do a better job of advertising your weaknesses than your strengths? Did you accidentally advertise what you do least instead of best?

If from your results you think you're marketing the wrong USP and losing business because your market has the wrong perception of you, then change it!

These are not minor decisions for you and your company to make. These can be "make-it or break-it" decisions. The good thing is you can survey your market. Track the results of sales and make necessary changes. These decisions are critical to building a HIGH-PROFIT business.

Communicate any changes to your market. A well stated USP is how to accomplish this.

Getting Into The Minds Of Your Prospects

So, how do you get into your prospects' minds?

You find or create your own position and communicate it over and over again to the right target market.

Here is something you must remember when marketing your company, *(almost no one does)*:

Be perceived by the public as differing from your competition!

Your prospects must see you as having something different, something special that sets you apart from the others in your industry. Otherwise, there's no reason for them to call you. They may call your competition or they may decide not to call anyone.

To the general public everybody in your industry may seem all the same. You know that's not true. Good positioning finds and communicates what's different about you. What sets you apart from others that do the same work as you do? Determine what makes you unique, your differences, so the uninformed public will know how they will benefit by doing business with you.

Now, the next thing in determining your strategic position is to discover and communicate these things:

· Who you are

· What you do

· Why you're different

· How you can benefit your prospects

There should be many differences between you and others doing the same work. If there aren't then you're not paying close enough attention or you need to invent some unique things that others don't do.

Some examples might be:

· Open weekends and evenings

· Special financing options

· New breakthrough equipment

· No premium for after hours work

· Family owned for 25 years

· Specializing in _____

· Great guarantees

· Something for FREE (that perhaps the rest of the industry charges for)

The next thing you want to make note of are all the benefits of doing business with your company. A benefit is an answer to your customer's question of *"What's in it for me?"*

People will not use you unless they get some benefit. You have to clearly and succinctly tell and show them how they will benefit by doing business with you.

Benefits do <u>not</u> include things like:

· We really care

· Locally owned and operated

· Friendly service

These things don't really say what you'll do for someone. They are vague and unspecific.

Some examples of benefits might be:

· We guarantee to save money on your _____ costs

· Deadline promises kept or we pay you — guaranteed

· We guarantee you'll get same day quotes

After you come up with benefits, ask some of your customers what benefits they have gotten from your relationship.

In trying to list the benefits of doing business with their company, many owners end up with a list of *features* instead of *benefits*. Just remember a feature is an item or facet of your product or service. A benefit is what that feature will DO for someone.

You need to see what people get out of buying your products or services. What do they end up with when it's all said and done? Do you ever get compliments/comments from your customers? How can you translate those into benefits? Keep your focus. Really see things from the eyes of your customers. You not only have to listen to what they say about you being unique and how you uniquely solve their problems, but also use the language they would use to describe that uniqueness.

Know the benefits you can give prospects and to communicate this to them. When you speak to prospects or customers, you must speak in customer language. You must have the viewpoint of the consumer and talk in terms the consumer understands. Think of it this way. If your best customer were to tell someone else why they do business with you, what would they say?

Now, write down the answer to the question:

How is your business (and you) better and different from who you compete with?

What does this mean? I want you to list how you think you are better than others in your industry. What do you feel your strengths are? Very few can be good at all things and if you were, no one would believe you anyway. But for now, list all the ways you think you are better. Remember here you want to tell your prospects how you differ from others in your profession without bad-mouthing or slamming the other guy.

If you say, "and I've done this and I've done that and I've done the next thing ... I can do all these things for you," soon you're the jack-of-all-trades. Jack-of-all-trades and master of none is what your market will think.

Look at it from your public's viewpoint:

· Are there ways you give better service than others?

· Are you more experienced in certain areas?

· Are you more personal?

· Do you have better guarantees or better payment options?

· Do you have better equipment?

You might think that it's too much work to create your USP. Believe me, it's not if you want a profitable business. The only reason your public is uninformed about the benefits of doing business with you is because YOU haven't informed them.

Now you're done with most of the research for your USP. We're ready to put all this information into a format you can use. You've probably already found a few new things to promote your business. Write a paragraph of around 20-50 words, the fewer the better, that uses the best differences and benefits from your research. Communicate with no hype who you are, what you do, why you're different and how you can benefit your prospects and customers. *Don't say, "We are the most experienced in town", your public never believes it.* What you want to say is, "We've been providing quality service for 25 years." The 25 years is the hidden proof of your experience.

"We really care" turns into "Our focus is on making sure every customer gets exactly what they want, when they want it — every time or it's free."

Finally - when creating your USP, you want to remember emotion. Most people justify their purchase with logic, but they make the purchase with emotion. They want to do business with you because you make them feel smart, or good about the decision. They need logical facts to back up the emotional decision they made. Don't lose sight of this, it's very important.

In summary:

· Make a list of every possible way a person could benefit from doing business with you. Your USP should state the biggest benefit and most unique benefit your prospects will get from doing business with you.

· Keep it short. Your USP should be only three sentences long - one sentence is best. Keep chipping away at it. Eliminate all dead weight. Don't stop until you have a crystal clear, concise, powerful USP you can put into action.

Take the time to create a compelling USP that appeals to your prospects and customers. It will become the cornerstone of your business and it will drive every aspect of your marketing.

Finally, when you have written your USP, e-mail it at bricar@marketownership.com. I will help you with some suggestions on how you can use your USP to market your company.

Some Typical USPs

In every item that follows the comparison is to the bulk of your competitors' services or products.

- Faster service

- Better prices or better value for the price

- Specialized products

- Wider selection

- More convenient location

- Fresher or newer products

- Nicer workers

- More honest business practices

- More comfortable surroundings

- Longer hours

- More experience

- Some special connection to customers (like a kosher grocery in an orthodox Jewish neighborhood)

- More fashionable

- More knowledgeable

- "Hand-made," "home-made" or "home grown"

- Better reviews

- Healthier

- Online shopping

- Other services such as repair or classes or customization

- More family friendly

- More creative

- More accessible

- More responsive

- Anything else people value

"In the business of referrals, trust is the most important reason a recommendation is made and, conversely, lack of trust the single greatest reason referrals don't happen.."

John Jantsch

9

The Best Marketing System Of All

How to Develop an Effective Referral Generating System to Grow Your Business

The quickest, easiest, most cost-effective way to grow a business is by installing an effective referral program that rewards your onboard clients for referring others to you.

Word of mouth, or buzz marketing, is the most cost efficient (it's free) and best form of marketing a business can use.

Businesses that rely on traditional commercial advertising are at the mercy of those who sell the advertising time or space, the prices they charge, and the results those ads produce. In this advertising the cost of the ad is the same whether it produces one response, ten responses, or a hundred responses; and it costs the same whether it produces one dollar in sales, ten dollars, or a hundred dollars.

Referral Programs Can Be "Zero-Risk"

Well crafted referral programs will only require payment when an actual client is developed. It's a true "pay-for-results" system, and is totally "Zero-Risk."

When traditional print ads don't work, common responses from ad salespeople are the ad must be run multiple times to create top of mind awareness, the ad must be larger, it must be placed in a different (more costly) location, or that it needs color… all of which add to the cost of the advertisement.

But well designed referral programs are based on newly acquired clients and not on increased spending. You only pay for results.

With traditional advertising, you pay with cash. But with referrals, often, the rewards, incentives or gifts you "pay" your referrers with can be your own products or services you either make, produce, or provide yourself, or that you buy at wholesale prices. The value to the referrer is the retail price of the product or service.

People will not refer others to a business unless they have received value from the products or services they purchased from the business, or unless they have experienced great service from that business. The more you can do for your customers or clients to give them a WOW! experience, the more likely they are to return to do business with you, and the more likely they are to refer others to you.

Begin With The End In Mind

If you know that referrals are gotten with exceptional service and an outstanding experience, then provide that service and those experiences, and referrals from your thrilled customers and clients is almost a given.

You'll find that not only will the number of referrals you generate increase, but so will the loyalty of your current customers and clients, which translates to more immediate profits. When your client base increases, not only do your profits and cash flow increase, but so does the commercial or resale value of your business.

How To Develop An Effective Referral Program

Here is a simple step-by-step cost-efficient way to increase the size of nearly any business.

1. Provide the best quality products and the most outstanding service to be found in your market. Do something either your competition cannot do, or they are not willing to do. Set yourself apart. Be unique and special. If you can't differentiate yourself by the products you sell, then differentiate yourself by the service you provide. Create a demand for whatever it is you offer. When people experience the benefits of an incredible product or outstanding service it is natural they want to tell others about it. Let it be you they talk about.

2. Let your customers or clients know, both verbally and by showing them, that you appreciate them and their business. Develop a simple script to invite them to refer other people they know to do business with you.

3. Develop a multi-tiered program based on the number of new clients your referrals generate, and reward your referrers in two ways: immediate gratification and delayed gratification. For instance:

Level	New Clients	Reward
Silver	4	Dinner for two, 5% discount on all products and services you sell.
Gold	8	Concert tickets, 10% discount on all products and services you sell.
Platinum	12	Night stay in local resort, 15% discount on all products and services you sell.
Diamond	15	Weekend get-away including flight and hotel, plus 20% discount on all products and services you sell.

In this example, the immediate gratification is a one-time payoff such as the dinner, concert tickets, the night in a local resort and the weekend get-away.

The delayed gratification is an ongoing benefit designed to keep your clients coming back. In our example, it is the discount your clients receive on their purchases.

In either case, your imagination is the only limiting factor in determining what you can offer your clients. Just remember to reward them for the NEW CLIENTS you generate... not the number of people they tell to contact you. If they get some nice rewards, they need to do their fair share of the conversion process.

4. Using the table below, determine what the average Annual Value and the average Lifetime Value of your clients is. How much on average, does each client spend with you each year and over the course of their "buying lifetime" with you? (Appendix A explains each line.)

A	Number of clients you currently have	
B	Amount of average sale	$
C	Average profit margin of each sales transaction	%
D	Average dollar amount of profit on each transaction (B x C)	$
E	Number of sales per year per client	
F	Average annual <u>revenue</u> value of each client (B x E)	$
G	Average annual <u>profit</u> value of each client (D x E)	$

H	Number of years client does business with you	
I	Lifetime <u>Revenue</u> Value of each client (F x H)	$
J	Lifetime <u>Profit</u> Value of each client (G x H)	$
K	Number of your clients who would like to receive FREE gifts, special rewards and VIP recognition	
L	Percentage of your clients who would refer others to you and in return receive FREE gifts, special rewards and VIP recognition (K ÷ A x 100)	%
M	If the percentage of your clients in Line "L" refer only _____ clients to you, you will grow your business by (L x number of new clients they refer)	%
N	Number of <u>new</u> clients you will generate (A x L)	
O	<u>Total</u> number of clients you will have (A x L + A)	
P	Additional annual revenue your business will generate (N x B x E)	$
Q	Additional annual profits your business will generate (N x D x E)	$

R	Total Lifetime Revenue Value (I x O)	$
S	Total Lifetime Profit Value (J x O)	$

5. Now that you know how much a client is "worth" to you over their "lifetime" of doing business with you, you can determine how much you will spend on a client who refers several clients to you.

Referrers From "L" in above table	Silver (4 New Clients) Growth in Business	Gold (8 New Clients) Growth in Business	Platinum (12 New Clients) Growth in Business	Diamond (15 New Clients) Growth in Business
10%	40%	80%	120%	150%
25%	100%	200%	300%	375%
50%	200%	400%	600%	750%
75%	300%	600%	900%	1125%
100%	400%	800%	1200%	1500%

6. Ask yourself this question: "Which would you rather have, a client who spends twice as much with you or a client who refers 4 others to you?"

7. When your business grows, you as the business owner benefits and the commercial or resale value of your business

increases. But don't neglect those who make it all happen... your team members.

You've developed a system to reward your clients for referring others to you, now construct a system that will reward your employees and team members to administer the referral program. If you can make your team members think and act as if they owned the business, then let them share in the rewards, they'll be more excited about working your systems.

Your employee incentive program can be as simple as movie passes or dinner certificates if they meet certain goals, or it can be more elaborate and be modeled after the same rewards you've outlined for client referrals. Just remember to be generous with your rewards. Your team members are very much responsible for your personal and business success.

Appendix A

An explanation of the Lifetime Value Calculator

A. **Number of clients you currently have** – The total number of clients on your books, in your database, or that regularly buy from you.

B. **Amount of average sale** – The money <u>on average</u> spent in every sales transaction.

C. **Average profit margin of each sales transaction** – The <u>average</u> percentage of profits you earn on each sale.

D. Average dollar amount of profit on each transaction (B x C) – The <u>average</u> number of dollars in profits you earn on each sales transaction.

E. Number of sales per year per client – The <u>average</u> number of times each client buys from you each year.

F. Average annual <u>revenue</u> value of each client (B x E) – This is gross income or revenue each client brings to your business in a year.

G. Average annual <u>profit</u> value of each client (D x E) – The profit dollars each client is worth to your business each year.

H. Number of year's client does business with you – This is how long a client does business with you before stopping or finding other options.

I. Lifetime <u>Revenue</u> Value of each client (F x H) – The number of gross revenue dollars each client brings to your business over their "lifetime" of doing business with you.

J. Lifetime <u>Profit</u> Value of each client (G x H) – The number of profit dollars each client brings to your business over their "lifetime" of doing business with you.

K. Number of your clients who would like to receive FREE gifts, special rewards and VIP recognition – Your best guess how many of your clients would like to participate in a reward or recognition program. Not all clients will. Some would prefer to buy quality products or services from you, be treated well, and left alone. And others like attention, recognition and rewards.

L. **Percentage of your clients who would refer others to you and in return receive FREE gifts, special rewards and VIP recognition (K ÷ A x 100)** – This reflects the percentage of your clients who would participate in recognition and rewards compared to your total of clients.

M. **If the percentage of your clients in Line "L" refer only _____ clients to you, you will grow your business by (L x number of new clients they refer)** – Here's where you can have fun. Experiment with the number of referrals you think your clients would refer to you, and watch what happens to the figures that follow.

N. **Number of <u>new</u> clients you will generate (A x L)** – This is the number of <u>new</u> clients you will generate based on the number of referrals your clients will refer to you.

O. **<u>Total</u> number of clients you will have (A x L + A)** – This is the total number of clients you will end up with if your current clients refer the number you thought they would.

P. **Additional annual revenue your business will generate (N x B x E)** – This is additional gross income (revenue) your business will generate in one year because of adding these new clients.

Q. **Additional annual profits your business will generate (N x D x E)** – Additional profits you will earn from your business in one year because of adding these new clients.

R. **Total Lifetime Revenue Value (I x O)** – The amount of gross income or revenue your business will generate from your newly expanded client base over the course of their "lifetime" of doing business with you.

S. **Total Lifetime Profit Value (J x O)** - The amount of profits your business will generate from your newly expanded client base over the course of their "lifetime" of doing business with you.

"The aim of Marketing is to make selling superfluous."

Peter Drucker

10

Four Marketing Strategies that Bring in a Flood of Business

Strategies that Work No Matter How Bad the Economy Sucks

The bottom line of all businesses is to make a profit. That's why a business exists. It sounds nice for someone to say the reason they're in business is to help other people, or to provide some needed service, but the real bottom line is the business owner wants and needs to realize a profit on his or her investment.

Profits drive businesses and allow them to provide more goods and services, create more jobs and expand the economy. Profits allow the philanthropist to continue giving and providing relief and humanitarian service to others.

Many factors affect profits, mainly because customers purchasing goods and services provided by the business. Without customers making purchases, there simply would not be a business.

If a business expects to remain in business for any length of time, or to grow, the business owner must master the skill of getting customers to do business with them.

That includes new customers... those with whom they have never done business before; current or existing customers... those who patronize the business regularly; and past customers...those who have done business before, but may have taken their business elsewhere.

Getting people to do business with you is called "marketing." Unfortunately, for many businesses, this process, although critical to the success of the business, is one of the tools business owner's least understand.

Marketing... *effective* marketing... the kind that produces inquiries about your offer, adds customers and increases your profits, is not just a matter of placing ads in the newspaper or sending out some mailings.

And it's not creating a beautiful brochure that describes the company, the president and the products and services offered by your business.

Results-producing marketing... the kind you want for your business... is a combined and coordinated effort of several factors.

But what about the economy? Doesn't that have something to do with how a business approaches marketing?

It certainly does, there's no question about it. The economy, and how it's performing, has a real impact on businesses and how they should approach their marketing efforts. And here's where many businesses get in trouble.

When the economy is down, most businesses stop, or drastically slow down their marketing efforts.

Then, without new customers coming on board, existing customers making repeat or additional purchases, and past customers returning, the company's business drops off even further.

Fewer customers making purchases automatically translates into less profits. Less profits means less available funds for marketing, and before you know it; a vicious cycle develops with a downward trend.

When times are tough, is not the time to cut back on your marketing efforts. Sure, other businesses do it. But people still have the need or the want for your products and services.

So, when other businesses are cutting back, that's the ideal time for you to forge ahead, and increase your marketing efforts. It's the one time you will have the least competition for your customer's attention.

When times are good... when the economy is booming, good marketing... effective marketing can blow the socks off your competition.

Why?

Because your competition doesn't understand the difference between the marketing they've always used, and high-impact marketing that's accountable and produces results. And if they keep on doing the marketing they've always done, and you move on to more effective types of marketing, they don't stand a chance.

Marketing can comprise many forms. Some involve money, some involve personnel and some involve a certain commitment of time. Some work well in good economic times, and others work better in a down economy.

Here are four good, useable marketing efforts that work well in any economic climate. These strategies can be put to work in your business today, and help move your business forward regardless of the economy or your available financial resources.

Marketing Strategy #1

"Do what you do so well, that when others see you do it, they want to see you do it again, and will bring others to see you do it."

That quote comes from Walt Disney. It was the strategy he used marketing Disneyland, and he said it could apply to any business, regardless of what the business sold or offered.

Broken down to its individual components, it means this:

"Do what you do...." That's what *you* do... not what anyone else does. It's important you do the things you (or your business) does the best. While it's okay to emulate other successful businesses and copy traits that made them successful, you should adopt those traits, add your own personality and adapt them to your business.

Do what you do... *"so well...."* That means excellence...not mediocrity. If you're going to do something in business, do it with excellence. No longer is it possible to maintain...long-term, a competitive advantage because of your product or the price you charge. We live in a "me-too" world, where your customers can buy the same or very similar products to what you offer from many other suppliers for the same or less money. You must do what you do well.

"...when others see you do it...." "Others" means your customers...the people who buy your products and/or services. When they see you do what you do (or buy what you sell, or deal with your company)... they,

"...want to see you do it again...." We call that, "repeat business." Your offer was so good, or the way you dealt with your customers was so unique, that they want to come back for more... to see you do it again. Not only that, but they will...

"...bring others to see you do it." That's called "referral business." When your customers like what you do and bring others to experience it, that business costs you nothing in hard marketing costs. It's a result of word-of-mouth. It's a personal endorsement of your products or services from a satisfied user. That's the sincerest form of flattery, and the best form of advertising you can get.

You're not trying to "meet" your customer's expectations... you want to "exceed" them... to give them more than they expected. Similar products and services can all be expected to perform in similar fashion. But for the attention, care and service we receive, we all have our perceptions of what "good" means.

Keep in your mind a balance scale. On one side of the scale mentally put the dollar amount you charge for your products and services.

On the other side of the scale, your service. Make sure the "service" of the scale always outweighs the "price" side. Be sure you always give more service than the customer perceives they should get from their transaction with you.

Here are a few questions to ask yourself that will help you determine how well you're doing:

- Do I offer the best quality product or service I can?

- What can I do to improve it?

- What is the best benefit to my customers that each of my products or services must offer?

- How can I better convey that to my customers?

- What can I offer my customer above and beyond the product or service they purchased?

- Do my customers trust the advice and suggestions they get from my staff, and do they feel comfortable dealing with us?

- Why should they do business with my establishment instead of any and all options they have, including doing nothing?

- Would I purchase this product or service if I were in the market for it?

- Would I purchase it from my company if I didn't own, or work for the company?

- Would I feel comfortable referring my friends, relatives and associates to this company?

The answers to these questions can help you determine where you need to make changes that will benefit both you and your customers, and add substantially to your bottom line.

Marketing Strategy #2

Use the testimonials of other satisfied customers to help pre-sell your prospects.

Testimonials are one of the most powerful tools any business owner can use, but also one of the most under-utilized.

Testimonials are not limited to any one type of advertising or promotional media. Television ads, radio announcements, newspaper layouts and infomercials all make use of testimonials.

Often, celebrities are used to promote certain products, especially when national or large-scale exposure is involved, but that's not always necessary.

Your own clients are some of the best sources of endorsement you could possibly want. Especially if those you are marketing to know them or if they have something else in common... perhaps they live in the same town, have similar businesses, belong to the same organization or association, etc.

There are only three reasons people don't buy from you.

1. They have no use for your product or service.
2. They can't afford your product or service.
3. You haven't developed the level of trust, credibility, and believability they need in you to do business with you.

There's not much you can do if a prospect can't use or pay for your services. But there is a lot you can do to help wipe away the underlying layers of skepticism they bring to the relationship and establish the trust level they need to say "Yes" to your offer.

People don't like to be the first to do anything... especially if it involves parting with their hard-earned money. And, they don't like to be manipulated. The sales world is full of hype and promotion, and often, false and misleading sales messages.

If your customer or prospect can see others have done what they are being asked to do, or others are doing it, they feel safe, and will be more likely to participate. But you first must relieve any nervousness they may have of being "taken."

Testimonials are easy to get. One of the most effective ways is to send users of your products or services a questionnaire or evaluation form that asks for their feedback on how they've benefited from using the product or service. You can send your survey by mail or have them fill out one online.

The questions should be in "open-ended" form, and ask for them to write their *feelings* about their experience with your product or the service they received from you, and not just for "yes" or "no" answers.

Another effective method is to call your clients on the telephone and record the conversation (with their permission).

Then you can transcribe the parts you want to use, and send a copy to them for their approval and authorization.

Often, after a brief warm up conversation, people will forget the tape is running, open up and give you good, useable information that can be edited for use as a testimonial.

Using testimonials is one of the most effective ways you can eliminate fear, increase the believability and credibility of your offer, and add to the number of sales or inquiries to your advertisements or promotions. Whatever you do, don't overlook this important and valuable tool!

Marketing Strategy #3

Build a database of current, past and prospective customers and keep in touch regularly.

Who are your current customers? Do you know? How do you know? Do you have a record that shows who they are, what products or services they regularly purchase, their last purchase, when it was, and how often they make purchases from you?

How do you know the person you consider a "current" customer isn't a "past" customer? When was the last time he or she bought from you? Have they sent any referrals to you lately? If so, who? If not, why not? Have they taken their business down the street to a competitor? If so, to whom? And why?

What about your prospective customers? Do you know who they are? Have you developed an "Ideal Customer Profile" that accurately describes who your best customers are so you'll know whom to target with your marketing efforts? Do you have a list of them? Do you know how to reach them? Are you reaching them regularly?

The answers to these questions can give you valuable information that can blast your business to never dreamed of heights.

By knowing exactly whom you have dealt with in the past, who you deal with, and who you would like to deal with can dramatically change your business, your profits and your bottom line.

If you're not using a computer to keep track of these and other categories of customers, you should be. This database can be the starting point of unbelievable profits!

Targeting your marketing efforts to the right people can make or break your entire advertising or marketing campaign. And if you're a small business, you can't afford to have that happen often. It'll drive you right out of business!

Keeping in touch with your customers…past, current and

prospective, is one of the best marketing tools you can employ. It need not be "hard-sell." It can be as simple as any of these examples:

- Send birthday cards to your clients.

- Send postcards on the anniversary date of their first purchase with you.

- Send a questionnaire asking for their evaluation of the product or service they purchased, or feedback on how it could be made better.

- Send an informational newsletter regularly.

- Involve your customers in a contest or promotion... perhaps a referral generating promotion.

- Sponsor client luncheons with guest speakers that address subjects of interest to your clients. Have them bring a friend.

- Send announcements of "preferred customer" sales or events by special invitation. Include an invitation for someone who is not one of your current customers.

Make your current customers feel special. Make your past customers feel missed

And make your prospective customers feel wanted.

Use your internal database to keep in touch with these groups of customers. Let them all know how much you care, and how much you appreciate their business, and this will take your business to new levels faster than nearly any other method you can think of.

Marketing Strategy #4

Make all of your advertising efforts "Direct-Response."

Nearly every advertisement or promotion you see today is what's known as "institutional" or "image" advertising. The ads promote the image of a particular product, service or institution.

Now, here's a hard and cold fact: People… your customers… couldn't care less about you or your image, your company or its image, your sales quotas, or whether or not you'll be in business this time next month. Not, at least, until you show them how your product or service can benefit them.

Image advertising may be okay for very large organizations that just want to create or maintain name recognition in the marketplace, but if you own a small or mid-size business, you most likely can't afford that luxury. Make every dollar you spend on promotions count.

The best way to do that is with "direct-response" advertising. This advertising focuses on the customer or prospect, and shows them how to solve their problems with your products or services.

Direct-response advertising gets your customers or prospects to become emotionally involved and to take a certain action… such as, call for more information, send in a response card or make a direct purchase.

With institutional ads, you have no way of knowing how effective your ads are because you have no way of measuring how many people respond to them.

So, you have no way of calculating the actual cost of the ad. That's not good.

Because direct-response ads require a person to take a specific action, they have an automatic built-in method of measurement, and you can measure whether it is profitable to run the ad again, or if it needs to be changed to be more effective.

Direct-response ads can be integrated effectively into the marketing efforts of nearly any business, and can take the form of mail order, newspapers, magazines, radio, TV, Internet and telemarketing.

Each of the components of a direct-response ad can be measured and tested separately so you can determine which combination of headline, opening statement, body copy, offer, guarantee, P.S., etc. works best.

Here are three simple, but not conclusive guidelines that can help you get the most from your direct-response ads:

- Create an attention-getting, emotional-based, benefit-oriented headline.

- Start small and test each component separately. Only increase the size of the ad gradually as you determine which combinations work the best.

- Offer a free gift for responding. Make sure the offer has a highly perceived value to the reader, listener or viewer. Consider things such as special reports, eBooks, free CD/DVD, booklets, introductory seminars or initial consultations.

Remember, the only reason you ever run an ad… any ad, is to evoke an immediate and qualified response from your customers or prospects.

You want and need this feedback, and you need it now, not six months from now. How else are you going to know if you should continue running this ad, or change some component of it?

You're in business to make a profit, not just to tell others about your wonderful products or services. Your ads have to work. They *must* work. They must produce results that can be translated into dollars.

That's the entire reason you run them. That's the entire reason you're in business.

Change your advertising efforts from a cost into an investment… a *profitable* investment with a measurable return, by changing all your advertising and promotional efforts to direct-response. It can add significantly to your bottom line, and will be one of the best moves you can make.

Conclusion

Marketing… effective marketing need not be difficult to be productive. But it must be done. If you fail to market, or if you market ineffectively, you can't expect to remain in business long, let alone grow your business.

With the tremendous increases in technology, and labor and materials available, more businesses are finding it difficult to maintain any competitive advantage because of their products or prices. For your business to prosper and grow, you need to aggressively engage in effective marketing practices.

If the products and services you offer to your customers and prospects are worthy of their hard-earned money… if they really will benefit them… then you, as a business owner, owe it to yourself, your employees, your suppliers and your customers to learn as much as you can about the marketing strategies that work in today's competitive business environment.

You then have an obligation to see that people take advantage of the wonderful benefits your products and services can provide for them. And, you have an obligation to do it as cost-effectively as possible so more people can afford them and your business can remain in business to serve even more people.

Now you've learned four strategies that can be implemented immediately and help you get on the road to making your business more successful and profitable.

Study them. Tailor them to fit your operation. Then apply them. They won't do you or anyone else any good unless you put them to work.

Finally, learn all you can about results-producing, lead-generation marketing. Become a student. Apply the concepts and strategies to your business, and watch it grow!

If you don't have the time or desire to learn the latest marketing techniques, don't just drop the ball. Your business and your customers are too important.

Find a qualified consultant that can help you analyze your business, decide which strategies will work best for you, then set in motion a systematic plan that will help you skyrocket your business to the next level. These four strategies will start you on your way. Apply them in your business, and your competition **won't stand** a chance!

"Do unto others as you would have done unto you."

The Holy Bible

11

The Most Powerful Business Concept of All?

Using the Golden Rule to Propel Your Business to the Top

What I am about to tell you, if you listen, could be the difference between massive success or just barely getting by in your business.

This powerful, universal principle has been around since man first walked on earth. This foundational anchor of life is the key to success in all areas of your life – not just business.

I am talking about the Golden Rule – do unto others as

you would have done unto you.

All of nature revolves around the Golden Rule. This strange rule of life is something we find hard to imagine. Give and you will receive is against our ego, yet the fact remains if we want more of something we must give to get.

Want more money? Give it away first. Want more love in your life? Give love first. Want to succeed? Help someone else become successful.

It is the law of cause and effect in action. It's also known as the law of sowing and reaping and the law of reciprocity. You need to know only that it works.

No one really knows why, but it does.. If you've tried it, as I have, the results are astounding – sometimes in amazing, unbelievable ways.

In business, the Golden Rule should be your foundation, your bedrock, and your guidepost to a better way of doing things.

How can you apply this into your own business? It isn't as hard as it sounds.

- Genuinely help others to become wealthy and you will become wealthy.
- Do whatever you can to help your colleagues and they will do the same for you.
- Be fanatically loyal to your clients and they will be fanatically loyal to your firm.
- Give without an expectation of return and you will receive without an expectation of return.
- Always approach a business situation with how can I help the other person get what they want

Counterintuitive I know. It goes against everything that little gremlin known as the ego believes.

Suppress the ego for the Golden Rule to work in your life and your business.

The ego tells you resources are limited and you have to follow what every other business in your field is doing just to compete – not true.

If you give – in value, quality and fair price – you can't help but watch your business succeed. It's a natural law and natural laws can never be broken.

Stop coming from a place of lack and scarcity in your business. Provide tremendous value and service to your clients, with exceptional customer service and success is practically assured.

What you give back comes back. Use it to your advantage and only send out value, kindness, loyalty and caring. Do that and you'll receive them back, tenfold.

You must come from a place of integrity in your business if you want to last in business.

If you make a mistake, own up to it. Don't hide behind excuses. Treat everyone with respect, including employees. Keep your word. Do what you say you will do. Be honest and trustworthy because if the client gets to know, like and trust you, then you have a client for life.

In this day and age of social media and the Internet, if you don't approach your business with 100 percent integrity, you'll be found out and the world will know about it in a blink of an eye through a blog or Facebook post, Tweet or forum discussion.

And just like that, millions of people are told not to do business with you. Not fun.

Be smart and don't get near the slippery slope. Maintain integrity in all your business dealings and use the power of the Golden Rule to propel you and your business to unimaginable success.

If you hoard what you have, the universe will keep its gifts from you. Sowing and reaping - cause and effect. Even if you're not a religious person and have no belief in God, this principle still applies. Look around, open your eyes and see, the law is everywhere working its magic.

Relationships come about when two people share souls with each other. To earn a living you have to deliver a certain service and your employer gives you money. If you have your own business and can't serve (give) properly, you'll be looking for a j-o-b quickly.

All progress is give and take, sowing and reaping. If people wouldn't invest or give of their time, money and talents, then life as we know it would cease to be. Hoarding and selfishness is against nature. The rain gives of itself and causes the grass, trees, plants and flowers to grow. They give shelter, food and joy to man and animal.

It's the reason we have what we have today. Without giving and receiving, man would still live in caves, afraid and crafting for himself a meaningless existence.

To receive the benefits of this timeless principle- just practice it. That's all there is to it. Give and you will receive. It cannot fail to reproduce after its kind. You must be a cheerful giver and a cheerful receiver for it to work magic in your life. If you complain after you give or feel guilty for receiving, you are diminishing its power.

Do you want abundance, love, harmonious relationships, a successful career and all this world has to offer? Start giving with joy and faith and watch amazing things happen in your life.

"When inspiration does not come to me, I go half way to meet it."

Sigmund Freud

Epilogue

Where Do You Go From Here?

Congratulations for making it this far. You have now been exposed to some of the most powerful and effective techniques, concepts and ideas available for succeeding in business.

But no matter how good these ideas are, just being exposed to them is not enough. You must also do something with them. For you to get the most value out of this material, consider developing a systematic action plan. An effective and results producing plan should comprise five areas:

1. EVALUATION

Ideas are nothing more than ideas until they are put into action. Once acted on, they have the potential to literally turn around a struggling business, or help an already successful business become even more dynamic and successful.

But before a person runs out and implements a new found idea, they should first take the time to evaluate their operation to determine just what areas are most lacking and could use the most attention.

You have the potential of making the most improvement in your own business, if you will take the time to identify and work on the area of greatest need, first.

2. RESEARCH

Once you've identified your greatest needs and placed them in priority order, you can search out solutions. Be on an opportunity lookout. The material in this book is just the beginning of the many places you can find good, usable, and practical ideas.

Don't turn any ideas away just because you think they might not pertain to your business or the way you operate. Capture them and then apply step number three.

3. PERSONALIZATION

As you encounter new ideas, keep an open mind. Study them. Analyze them. And think them through. Ask yourself if an application can be made to your specific situation by simply changing or modifying part of the concept or idea.

If a certain illustration uses a certain product or service for the example, but you don't sell that product or service, a simple adjustment might be all that's needed.

The material in the book illustrates concepts, and only uses certain types of products as examples to make various points.

4. IMPLEMENTATION

Just as a membership in a health club won't do its owner any good unless he or she goes to the club and participates in the exercise program, so too, with the information in this book.

It's of no practical use unless it is implemented. It's easy to come up with good ideas and develop plans, but where most people get bogged down is putting them into action. It's not always easy, but if you're going to truly succeed, you must do whatever it takes to act on your plans.

5. REVIEW

After you've worked with your new ideas for a period of time, stop and evaluate how things are working. You may need to make adjustments so you can continue to see improvement.

Sometimes, an idea you thought was great, doesn't work out. That's okay, don't continue using it. Just scrap it and move on to something else.

If you find an idea that works well, see if you can refine it, or "plus" it to make it even more effective.

That's all there is to it. Sounds simple enough to say, but in reality, there's a lot to do. The plain and truthful facts are most people simply won't take the time and effort to do the things we've just discussed. That's unfortunate on one hand, because they could be even more successful than they are now.

Their failure to take action is good for you. Because if it's you that does these things and not them, it will be you who realizes the success.

And don't forget to live the Golden Rule in all areas of your life, not just business.

Now you have the tools…

GO FOR IT!

MARKETING CHEATSHEET

The Five Primary Functions of Marketing

1. Lead Generation (Targeting and Differentiating-USP)
2. Lead Nurturing
3. Conversion
4. Repeat Business
5. Referrals

The Four Ways to Grow a Business

1. Get New Customers
2. Get Customers to Spend More
3. Get Customers to Buy More Often
4. Acquisitions or Upping LCV

Main Media for Lead Generation

1. TV
2. Radio
3. Newspapers
4. Magazines
5. Internet/Email
6. Mobile
7. Direct Mail

Lead Generation Bait

1. Ebook/Book
2. Free Report
3. Video Series
4. Email Series
5. Audio
6. White Paper
7. Software

Step-By-Step Internet/Offline Marketing Plan (Product or Service)

1) Decide who your target market is. Niche it down. (age, sex, live, buy, income, etc)
2) Find out what their biggest problem or greatest desire is
3) Create a product or service that solves their biggest problem or fulfills their greatest desire
4) Create the offer:
   A. Headline
   B. Deadline
   C. Scarcity or Urgency
5) Create free content to give away when they opt-in (ebook, video, reports)
6) Have a blog to give prospects free info to prove you're the bomb
7) Use free offers to build a master list you can market to over and over
8) Move prospects up the marketing funnel (Low price offers to high end)
9) Build your coaching or high ticket backend to sell to customers for more money
10) Keep marketing and create new products and services to your list
11) Use offline and online marketing strategies to get and convert traffic. (Get offline people online and online people offline)
12) Wash, rinse and repeat

CONTACT BRIAN
BRICAR@MARKETOWNERSHIP.COM

BRIAN'S BLOG
MARKETOWNERSHIP.COM

ABOUT THE AUTHOR

Brian Carson is an author, freelance sports writer and marketing consultant who is the marketing director and business development coordinator for Naylor & Associates. He has been happily with his wife, Maria, for 24 years.

Brian is the author of two books, **Customers for Life** and **The Four Pillars of Success**, and is working on two others. He has various websites across the Internet and currently lives in Central Pennsylvania with his wife.

www.ingramcontent.com/pod-product-compliance
Lightning Source LLC
Chambersburg PA
CBHW060609200326
41521CB00007B/708